BETTY CROCKER'S
Low-Calorie Cookbook

Director of Photography: Stephen Manville

Illustrator: Roland Rodegast

Golden Press/New York
Western Publishing Company, Inc.
Racine, Wisconsin

Pictured on the cover:
410-Calorie Dinner—
Chicken with Mushroom Gravy (page 21),
Easy Broiled Zucchini (page 44),
Melon Balls (½ cup)
with Fluffy Fruit Dressing (page 36, 1 tablespoon),
Lacy Melba Toast (page 64),
Pot de Crème (page 56).

First Printing, 1973

Library of Congress Catalog Card Number: 73-83923

Contents

Dear Calorie-Counter,

The secret of your success? Simple. Cutting calories in such a way that no one notices they're missing. The point is, calorie-counting shouldn't mean doing without. It should mean doing things differently. We're talking about a constant, not a sometime, thing. We're talking about planning differently, cooking differently, eating differently—and it's all easier than you'd believe. That's what this book is all about. How you can slim down, shape up, or simply hold the line and still enjoy foods you and your family love.

Would you believe salads shining with dressing, potatoes without guilt, desserts that look calorie-laden but aren't? You'll find dozens and dozens of recipes in these pages, each one pared—by a substitute ingredient, an alternate cooking method, a lesser amount of some ingredients, or any combination of these—to a new low in calories.

To start you off, we've put together menus guaranteed to be family-pleasers and calorie-counted for your convenience. In case yours is a house divided (as are most), there are hints on how to make one meal do for both calorie-counters and the rest of the family. And as an added bonus, we've suggested plans for putting our recipes together to make festive fare for your guests without breaking training for you.

There's a complete rundown of daily nutritional needs plus comparative calorie lists to show you where you're safe in "eating hearty" and where you'd better watch your step. And throughout the book we've sprinkled hints to help you out at calorie-counting stress points.

In short, we've tried to point you in the new direction. And once you've caught the spirit, we predict you'll want to branch out on your own. By using these guides to create your own dishes and your own special menus, we *know* you'll reap compliments for your food, and your family will be healthier and happier.

Sincerely,

Betty Crocker

YES YOU CAN!

That did it! What? An uncomplimentary remark about your weight, the sight of your not-trim self in a 3-way mirror? It hardly matters. What counts now is your determination to lose weight—starting *right now.* Congratulations—you've taken your first step in the right direction!

NOW LET'S BEGIN:

☐ Set a target date and start! Don't let anything deter you. The sooner you start, the sooner you'll be at your desired weight.

☐ Check with your doctor before you begin. Never cut calories to less than 1200 a day without a medical go-ahead!

☐ Set reasonable goals, never more than a pound or two a week. (Be realistic so you won't get discouraged!) And remember—not everybody can or should be a size 8.

☐ Find a friend who'll count calories with you. Sympathetic support is the dieter's greatest ally—besides, it will keep you from boring the rest of the world to death.

☐ Pose for three candid snapshots—front, side and back views. No matter how awful, keep them. Repeat the snapshot routine in 30 days as visual proof of the progress you've made.

☐ Memorize "What Is Meant by a Serving?" (page 7). The sizes of portions can make or break your diet. Get an inexpensive scale and weigh everything before you put it on your plate. (Not as tedious as it sounds—after a little while, you'll recognize too-big portions on sight.)

☐ Chart the essential food groups (page 7) and the number of daily servings you need of each. Keep track of everything you eat.

☐ Stock up on coffee, tea, low-calorie soda pop, instant bouillon, vegetable juices, nonfat dry and evaporated skim milk. Provision the refrigerator with vegetable snacks. These emergency rations can very well prove to be your survival kit.

☐ Get some graph paper to record your weekly weight loss—it's pure pleasure to watch it plummet. For more fun, mark in special rewards at certain loss levels—"2 pounds: Magazine subscription." "5 pounds: Theater tickets." "10 pounds: Brand-new outfit!" (You'll need it by then.)

☐ Always think thin. Good luck!

HOW MUCH CAN A CALORIE-COUNTER EAT EACH DAY?

Everyday variety is important. These are total servings, but they can be spread over breakfast, lunch and dinner according to your personal likes. Be sure that you include the servings required for each type of food every day—no more, no less.

Food	1200 Calories Daily	1500 Calories Daily
Meat, Fish, Poultry, Eggs	3 small servings (total 7 ounces cooked weight)	3 small servings (total 7 ounces cooked weight)
Fruits	2 servings	2 servings
Vegetables	2 servings	2 servings
Cereals, Breads	4 servings	5 servings
Milk	2 cups fortified skim milk	2 cups whole milk*
Extras	1 serving	3 servings

* If you're consuming 1500 calories a day and you drink skim milk, you can have a total of 7 servings in the Extras category.

HOW TO MAKE YOUR OWN DAILY CHECK-OFF CHART

Food	Breakfast	Lunch	Snack	Dinner	Required Servings
(List food groups above)	(Leave this space blank and check off servings in the right place as you eat them. Total the columns each day to see which foods you've missed.)				(List required servings above to fit your calorie needs.)

WHAT IS MEANT BY A SERVING?

Here are some examples. Each of these items is one serving:

Meat, Fish, Poultry, Eggs*
- ☐ ¼ pound (before cooking) boneless raw meat
- ☐ 2 slices (4 × 2¼ inches each) or 3 ounces cooked meat or fish
- ☐ 1 cooked hamburger, 3 × ½ inch
- ☐ 1 cooked small chicken leg and thigh

* 1 egg can be substituted for 1 ounce meat

Cereals, Breads
- ☐ 1 slice bread or small dinner roll
- ☐ 1 ounce ready-to-eat unsweetened iron-fortified cereal (about 1 cup)
- ☐ ½ cup cooked cereal
- ☐ ½ cup cooked rice, cornmeal, macaroni, noodles or spaghetti

Fruits, Vegetables
- ☐ 1 medium fruit (apple)
- ☐ 2 small fruits (apricots, prunes)
- ☐ ¼ cantaloupe
- ☐ 10 to 12 cherries or grapes
- ☐ 1 cup fresh berries
- ☐ ½ cup fresh, canned or frozen unsweetened fruit or juice
- ☐ ½ cup cooked vegetable
- ☐ 1 cup raw leafy vegetable

Milk
- ☐ 1 cup milk (8 ounces)

Extras
- ☐ 1 teaspoon butter, margarine or oil
- ☐ 1 teaspoon salad dressing
- ☐ 6 nuts (almonds, cashews, walnuts)
- ☐ 35 calories of another food

WHAT SHOULD A CALORIE-COUNTER CHOOSE?

	Choose	Avoid or Eat Sparingly
Meat, Poultry, Fish, Eggs	Very lean, well-trimmed meats Poultry and fish without skin Broiled or baked foods	Fatty meats, cold cuts, frankfurters Panfried or deep-fat fried foods
Vegetables	All vegetables: fresh, plain frozen or canned (eat less often: corn, kidney and lima beans, peas, potatoes, winter squash)	Vegetables in sauces or deep-fat fried
Fruits	Fresh, unsweetened canned fruits or juices; fruits rich in vitamin C (oranges, grapefruit, strawberries, cantaloupes)	Fruits in heavy syrup; fruit fritters
Cereals, Breads	Whole grain, enriched, re-stored or fortified cereals and breads	Muffins, pancakes, waffles, biscuits, doughnuts
Milk	Fortified skim, buttermilk, non-fat dry milk Dry or 2% creamed cottage cheese, farmer or pot cheese, Neufchâtel and other low-calorie cheeses	Whole milk Cream
Extras—only after you have your required servings (see page 7) in the groups above	Low-calorie gelatins Desserts made with skim milk Egg whites Low-calorie whips Cocoa powder Angel food cake Desserts in this book Popcorn without added fat Low-calorie jams, jellies, syrups Mock Mayonnaise (page 65) Butter, margarine, mayonnaise	Whipped cream Chocolate Fudge, caramels Most cakes Ordinary pies, cookies Fried or deep-fat fried snacks Jams, jellies, syrups Rich gravies, sauces

MARINATED CUBE STEAKS

4 beef cube steaks
  (about 4 ounces each)
¼ cup low-calorie blue cheese or
  Italian dressing

1 medium tomato, cut into eighths
Salt

Use large skillet with non-stick finish or coat regular skillet with vegetable spray-on for cookware. Place meat in skillet; pour dressing over meat. Cover and let stand 20 minutes, turning once.

Brown meat in skillet over medium-high heat about 4 minutes on each side. About 2 minutes before meat is done, add tomato. Season with salt. Serve meat topped with tomato and pan juices.

4 servings/250 calories each.

PARTY ROUND STEAK

2-pound beef round or family
  steak, 1 inch thick
1 can (4 ounces) mushroom stems
  and pieces, drained

¾ cup dry red or white wine
1 teaspoon salt
1 teaspoon lemon pepper

Diagonally slash outer edge of fat on meat at 1-inch intervals to prevent curling when meat cooks (do not cut into lean). Place meat and mushrooms in shallow baking dish. Mix wine, salt and lemon pepper; pour over meat. Cover and refrigerate 8 hours, turning meat 2 or 3 times.

Set oven control at broil and/or 550°. Place meat on rack in broiler pan. Broil with top 3 inches from heat 7 to 8 minutes on each side for medium-rare. Heat mushrooms and wine in small saucepan.

Trim fat from meat; cut meat diagonally into slices and serve topped with mushrooms and wine.

8 servings/185 calories each.

Meats and Main Dishes—The Hearty Heart of Your Meal

or

How to Make the Main Event Memorable

When anyone asks, "What's for dinner?" they really mean what meat or chicken or seafood is going to do the star turn at the meal. For this chapter, we've chosen bountiful dishes to delight the taste and still give you and your family vital protein, all the while whittling away at excess calories.

GINGER BEEF

This savory steak is very simple to make. Saving idea: Buy a chunk of gingerroot, freeze, and slice off pieces as you need them. Fresh ginger flavor—anytime.

2 **pounds beef round steak, ¾ to 1 inch thick**
2 **cloves garlic**
½ **teaspoon salt**
Dash pepper
1 **can (10½ ounces) condensed beef broth (bouillon)**
2 **tablespoons cornstarch**

¼ **cup water**
1 **tablespoon soy sauce**
¼ **teaspoon crushed gingerroot (1 thin slice) or ⅛ teaspoon ground ginger**
1 **package (7 ounces) frozen Chinese pea pods**
Hot Cooked Rice (below)

Trim fat from meat; cut meat into thin strips, 2 × ¼ inch. Peel garlic and make several cuts on one end of each clove to release flavor.

Use large skillet with non-stick finish or coat regular skillet with vegetable spray-on for cookware. Cook and stir garlic in skillet until brown. Remove garlic and discard. Brown meat in skillet over medium-high heat, stirring occasionally. Sprinkle with salt and pepper. Stir in broth; heat to boiling. Reduce heat and simmer uncovered until meat is tender, 10 to 15 minutes. (Add small amount of water if necessary.)

Mix cornstarch, water and soy sauce; stir into meat mixture in skillet. Cook, stirring constantly, until mixture thickens and boils. Boil and stir 1 minute. (Gravy will be thin.)

Stir in gingerroot and pea pods. Cook, stirring occasionally, until pea pods are crisp-tender, about 5 minutes. Serve on rice.

8 servings/220 calories each. (Each serving: ½ cup meat mixture, ½ cup rice.)

Hot Cooked Rice

For one of your daily cereal or bread servings, rice or noodles is a nice change of pace. Just be extra careful in measuring your portion.

2⅔ **cups boiling water**
1⅓ **cups uncooked regular rice**

1 **teaspoon salt**

Heat oven to 350°. Mix all ingredients thoroughly in ungreased 1- or 1½-quart casserole or in baking dish, 11¾ × 7½ × 1¾ inches. Cover tightly with aluminum foil and bake until liquid is absorbed and rice is tender, 25 to 30 minutes.

4 cups cooked rice/115 calories per half cup.

BEEF-TOMATO CURRY

½-pound beef flank or round steak,
  cut into ½- to ¾-inch pieces
1½ teaspoons instant beef bouillon
½ cup water
2 large tomatoes, peeled and cut
  into wedges (about 1½ cups)
1 green pepper, cut into 1-inch
  squares

2 medium onions, cut into wedges
1 teaspoon curry powder
1 tablespoon sugar
1 tablespoon cornstarch
1 tablespoon water
1 can (16 ounces) Chinese
  vegetables
¾ teaspoon salt

Use large skillet with non-stick finish or coat regular skillet with vegetable spray-on for cookware. Cook and stir meat and bouillon in skillet until meat is brown. Remove meat; set aside.

In same skillet, heat ½ cup water, the tomatoes, green pepper, onions, curry powder and sugar to boiling, stirring occasionally. Cover and cook over medium-high heat 3 minutes. Stir in meat; heat, stirring constantly, until hot, about 1 minute.

Mix cornstarch and 1 tablespoon water; stir into meat mixture. Cook, stirring constantly, until mixture thickens and boils. Boil and stir 1 minute. Keep warm over low heat. In saucepan, heat Chinese vegetables (with liquid) to boiling; drain and sprinkle salt on vegetables. Serve meat sauce on Chinese vegetables.

4 servings/155 calories each. (Each serving: about 1 cup meat mixture, ½ cup Chinese vegetables.)

Take advantage of tenderizers. The commercial ones, seasoned or unseasoned, let you broil lean, tougher meats beautifully.

BEAN SPROUT BURGERS

2 pounds lean ground beef
½ cup bean sprouts, coarsely
  chopped

½ cup water chestnuts, finely
  chopped
1¾ teaspoons salt
2 teaspoons soy sauce

Mix all ingredients thoroughly. Shape mixture into 8 patties, each about 3½ inches in diameter and ¾ inch thick.

Set oven control at broil and/or 550°. Place patties on rack in broiler pan. Broil with tops 3 inches from heat about 5 minutes on each side for medium burgers.

8 servings/190 calories each.

Pictured on page 40.

MEAT LOAF RING WITH TWIN BEAN FILLING

½ cup soft bread crumbs	¼ cup finely chopped green pepper
⅔ cup skim milk	⅓ cup chili sauce
1 egg	1 can (8 ounces) cut green beans
1¼ teaspoons salt	1 can (8 ounces) cut wax beans
1 pound lean ground beef	Lemon pepper
½ cup finely chopped onion	½ cup chili sauce
1 cup finely shredded carrot	

Heat oven to 350°. Use 5-cup ring mold or loaf pan, 8½ × 4½ × 2¾ inches, with non-stick finish, or coat regular ring mold or loaf pan with vegetable spray-on for cookware. Mix bread crumbs, skim milk, egg, salt, meat, onion, carrot, green pepper and ⅓ cup chili sauce thoroughly. Spread mixture in ring mold. Bake until done, about 1 hour. Drain off fat.

Heat green and wax beans (with liquid) to boiling; drain. Season with lemon pepper. Loosen meat from side of mold; unmold onto serving platter. Spread ½ cup chili sauce on top; spoon beans into center of ring or around loaf.

6 servings/240 calories each. (Each serving: 1/6 meat loaf, ⅓ cup beans.)

CHILI WITH YELLOW BEANS

Beef groundwork. Recipes in this book are based on lean ground beef. It costs a bit more, but shrinkage is less, and it contains up to 20% less fat than regular ground beef. You needn't add fat for cooking, either, if you use a Teflon-finish (non-stick) pan or coat your skillet with Pam vegetable spray-on for cookware. More fat-losing facts: Always drain any fat from meat while it's cooking; grilling or rack-broiling lets fat drip off and away.

1 pound lean ground beef	1 can (10¾ ounces) condensed
¼ cup chopped onion	tomato soup
1 can (16 ounces) tomatoes	¼ teaspoon pepper
1 can (16 ounces) cut wax beans, drained	1 teaspoon salt
	1 teaspoon chili powder

Cook and stir meat and onion in large skillet until meat is brown. Drain off fat. Stir in remaining ingredients; heat to boiling. Reduce heat; cover and simmer meat mixture 25 to 30 minutes.

6 servings/190 calories each. (Each serving: 1 cup.)

STUFFED GREEN PEPPERS

6 large green peppers
5 cups boiling water
1½ pounds lean ground beef
2 tablespoons chopped onion
1 teaspoon salt

⅛ teaspoon garlic powder
1 cup cooked rice
1 cup tomato juice
6 thick tomato slices

Cut thin slice from stem end of each pepper; remove all seeds and membranes. Cook peppers in boiling water 5 minutes; drain.

Heat oven to 350°. Cook and stir meat and onion in large skillet until meat is brown and onion is tender. Drain off fat. Stir in salt, garlic powder, rice and tomato juice; heat to boiling.

Lightly stuff each pepper with ½ cup meat mixture. Stand peppers upright in ungreased baking dish, 11¾ × 7½ × 1¾ inches. Cover with aluminum foil and bake 45 minutes. Top each pepper with a tomato slice and sprinkle with salt. Bake uncovered 15 minutes.

6 servings/255 calories each.

DO-IT-YOURSELF TACO FEAST

1½ pounds lean ground beef
1 envelope (1¼ ounces) taco
   seasoning mix
½ teaspoon salt
1 cup water
12 ready-to-serve taco shells
¾ cup shredded lettuce

¾ cup chopped tomato
¾ cup chopped green pepper
¾ cup chopped onion
¾ cup chopped cucumber
¾ cup shredded Cheddar cheese
Taco sauce

Cook and stir meat in large skillet until brown. Drain off fat. Stir in taco seasoning mix, salt and water; heat to boiling. Reduce heat and simmer uncovered 15 to 20 minutes, stirring occasionally. While meat simmers, heat taco shells on ungreased baking sheet in 350° oven 3 to 5 minutes.

Spoon ¼ cup meat mixture into each taco shell. Add 1 tablespoon each lettuce, tomato, green pepper, onion, cucumber and cheese. Top with taco sauce.

12 tacos/190 calories each.

Cool it. If you're tempted to nibble as you cook, keep a glass of ice water at hand and sip instead of tasting.

NO-NOODLE LASAGNE

Keep all the lush lasagne flavors, but cut the calorie cost drastically by substituting zucchini slices for noodles. The family will want seconds of this. Pictured on page 39.

1 pound lean ground beef
1 can (15 ounces) tomato sauce
1½ teaspoons garlic salt
1 teaspoon basil leaves
1 teaspoon oregano leaves
1 carton (12 ounces) dry cottage cheese (1½ cups)
¼ cup grated Romano cheese

1 egg
1½ pounds zucchini, cut lengthwise into ¼-inch slices
2 tablespoons flour
1 package (4 ounces) shredded mozzarella cheese
¼ cup grated Romano cheese

Heat oven to 350°. Cook and stir meat in large skillet until brown. Drain off fat. Stir in tomato sauce, garlic salt, basil leaves and oregano leaves; heat to boiling. Reduce heat and simmer uncovered until mixture is consistency of spaghetti sauce, about 10 minutes.

Use baking pan, 9 × 9 × 2 inches, with non-stick finish or coat regular baking pan with vegetable spray-on for cookware. Mix cottage cheese, ¼ cup Romano cheese and the egg. Layer half each of zucchini, flour, cottage cheese mixture, meat sauce and mozzarella cheese; repeat. Sprinkle ¼ cup Romano cheese on top. Bake uncovered 45 minutes. Let stand 20 minutes before serving. Cut into squares.

9 servings/240 calories each.

TOMATOED LIVER STRIPS

1 pound sliced beef liver, cut into 1-inch strips
1 teaspoon instant beef bouillon

½ small onion, sliced
½ cup tomato sauce or chili sauce

Use large skillet with non-stick finish or coat regular skillet with vegetable spray-on for cookware. Cook and stir meat and instant bouillon in skillet over high heat until meat is brown. Stir in onion and tomato sauce. Reduce heat; cover and cook over medium heat until meat is done, about 5 minutes.

4 servings/170 calories each with tomato sauce; 195 calories each with chili sauce.

CHINESE PORK TENDERLOIN SLICES

1-pound pork tenderloin	1½ teaspoons vinegar
¼ cup soy sauce	⅛ teaspoon pepper
1 tablespoon catsup	1 clove garlic, crushed

Cut meat lengthwise in half. Mix remaining ingredients in medium bowl. Add meat and turn to coat all sides. Cover and refrigerate, turning meat occasionally, at least 8 hours.

Place meat on rack in roasting pan and bake in 350° oven 50 minutes. Cut into ¼-inch slices. Serve immediately or wrap in aluminum foil and refrigerate (up to 4 days) or freeze and use as desired.

About 64 slices/15 calories each.

Nifty now-or-later meat. Marvelous marinated pork to serve sliced in Open-face Roast Pork Sandwiches (page 65) or cubed in Super Supper Salad (page 17).

PORK ROLL

1 teaspoon salt	4 cups water
½ teaspoon ground allspice	2 cups ½-inch slices celery
½ teaspoon pepper	1 tablespoon instant minced onion
½ teaspoon sage	2 bay leaves
3-pound rolled pork loin roast	6 peppercorns
6 whole cloves	6 whole allspice

Mix salt, ½ teaspoon allspice, the pepper and sage; rub on meat. Insert cloves in meat. Place meat and remaining ingredients in Dutch oven; heat to boiling. Reduce heat; cover and simmer 1½ hours, turning meat once or twice.

Remove from heat; leave meat in broth in Dutch oven. Cover meat with a plate; place a heavy weight on the plate (to press meat while it cools).

When cool, remove meat from broth and remove string. Cut meat into ¼-inch slices. Serve immediately or wrap in aluminum foil and refrigerate (up to 4 days) or freeze and use as desired. Strain broth into bowl; cover and refrigerate (up to 2 days) and use as desired.

About 22 slices/110 calories each.

Keep a cool but wonderfully aromatic kitchen by cooking a lean pork roast on top of the range. Press meat and slice for sandwiches; use skimmed broth for German-style Vegetable Soup (page 66) the next day.

PINEAPPLE PORK CHOPS

4 lean loin pork chops, ½
inch thick
1 can (8 ounces) sliced pineapple
in unsweetened pineapple juice,
drained (reserve 3 tablespoons
juice)

⅓ cup soy sauce
¼ teaspoon monosodium glutamate
¼ teaspoon garlic powder
Paprika
Parsley

Trim fat from chops. Place chops in ungreased baking dish, 8 × 8 × 2 inches. Mix reserved pineapple juice, the soy sauce, monosodium glutamate and garlic powder; pour over chops. Cover and refrigerate, turning chops once or twice, about 8 hours.

Heat oven to 350°. Top each chop with a pineapple slice; sprinkle with paprika. Cover tightly with aluminum foil and bake until done, about 45 minutes. Uncover and bake 5 minutes longer. Remove chops with pineapple slices to serving platter; garnish with parsley.

4 servings / 300 calories each.

BRAISED PORK TENDERLOIN PATTIES

4 pork tenderloin patties
(about 4 ounces each), ½
inch thick

2 teaspoons soy sauce
Garlic salt
1 to 2 tablespoons water

Use large skillet with non-stick finish or coat regular skillet with vegetable spray-on for cookware. Place patties in skillet; sprinkle each with ¼ teaspoon soy sauce and dash garlic salt and brown over medium-high heat. Turn; sprinkle each patty with ¼ teaspoon soy sauce and dash garlic salt and brown other side. Add water to skillet; cover and cook over low heat until patties are done, about 30 minutes. Serve meat with pan juices.

4 servings / 215 calories each.

The servings in this book are all reasonable portions for the calorie-counter. If you're cooking for a hungry family or guests as well, reckon on fewer servings per recipe, or double the recipe!

PORK TENDERLOIN CHOW MEIN

1-pound pork tenderloin
1 cup sliced celery
1 medium onion, chopped (about ½ cup)
3 tablespoons soy sauce
1 teaspoon monosodium glutamate
2 teaspoons instant beef bouillon or 2 beef bouillon cubes
2 cups water

2 tablespoons cornstarch
1 can (3 ounces) sliced mushrooms, drained (reserve ¼ cup liquid)
1 can (16 ounces) Chinese vegetables, drained
1 can (16 ounces) bean sprouts, rinsed and drained
½ teaspoon salt

Splits up splendidly—calorie-counters eat it served over bean sprouts, hungry family members heap it on crisp fried chow mein noodles. Pictured on page 38.

Cut meat into ½-inch slices, then cut slices into ¼-inch strips. Use large skillet with non-stick finish or coat regular skillet with vegetable spray-on for cookware. Cook and stir meat in skillet until brown. Stir in celery, onion, soy sauce, monosodium glutamate, bouillon and water. Cover and simmer 30 minutes.

Mix cornstarch and reserved mushroom liquid; stir into meat mixture. Stir in mushrooms and Chinese vegetables. Cook, stirring constantly, until mixture thickens and boils. Boil and stir 1 minute.

Sprinkle bean sprouts with salt and heat, stirring occasionally. Serve meat mixture on bean sprouts.

6 servings/200 calories each. (Each serving: scant 1 cup meat mixture, ⅓ cup bean sprouts.)

SUPER SUPPER SALAD

1 can (16 ounces) sauerkraut, drained (reserve liquid)
1 Bermuda onion, thinly sliced
2 dill pickles, cut into julienne strips

1 tart apple, pared and sliced
1⅓ cups diced cooked ham (about ½ pound)

In salad bowl, layer ⅓ each sauerkraut, onion slices, dill pickle strips, apple slices and meat. Repeat 2 times. Drizzle reserved sauerkraut liquid on top. Cover and refrigerate about 1 hour.

4 servings/105 calories each. (Each serving: 1 cup.)

VEAL CHARLOTTE

6 veal cutlets (4 ounces each) or 1½-pound veal round steak	⅓ cup water
2 teaspoons instant beef bouillon	2 teaspoons cornstarch
½ teaspoon paprika	1 teaspoon instant beef bouillon
1 pound mushrooms, sliced	⅛ teaspoon salt
½ teaspoon salt	1 cup water
¼ teaspoon garlic powder	Poppy Seed Noodles (below)
1 teaspoon grated lemon peel	Lemon wedges
1 tablespoon lemon juice	Parsley

Use large skillet with non-stick finish or coat regular skillet with vegetable spray-on for cookware. If using veal round steak, cut into 6 pieces and pound until each piece is ¼ inch thick. Sprinkle meat with 2 teaspoons bouillon and the paprika; brown in skillet over medium-high heat. Arrange mushrooms on meat. Mix ½ teaspoon salt, the garlic powder, lemon peel, lemon juice and ⅓ cup water; pour over mushrooms. Reduce heat; cover and simmer until meat is done, about 30 minutes. (If necessary, add small amount of water.)

Mix cornstarch, 1 teaspoon bouillon, ⅛ teaspoon salt and 1 cup water; stir into meat mixture. Heat to boiling, stirring constantly. Boil and stir 1 minute. Serve meat mixture on Poppy Seed Noodles and garnish with lemon wedges and parsley.

6 servings/310 calories each. (Each serving: meat, ⅓ cup mushrooms, 2 tablespoons gravy, ½ cup noodles.)

Poppy Seed Noodles

Heat 6 cups water and 1 tablespoon salt to boiling. Add 8 ounces medium noodles (4 to 5 cups); heat to boiling. Boil uncovered, stirring occasionally, 7 to 10 minutes; drain. Toss noodles with 2 teaspoons poppy seed.

Make more of mealtime than just eating. Set a pretty table and generate lively conversation. Give everyone something to think about besides the food.

SAUCY TURKEY ROLL

2- to 2½-pound turkey roast* (without gravy)	1 tablespoon soy sauce
½ cup rosé	½ teaspoon rosemary leaves
	½ teaspoon marjoram leaves

Bake turkey roast as directed on package except—before baking, mix remaining ingredients and pour onto roast. Cut roast into ½-inch slices and spoon 1 tablespoon pan juice on each slice.

About 10 slices/95 calories each.

* If turkey roast is in cello-bag and directions call for baking in bag, do not remove. Snip X with kitchen scissors in top of bag; pour remaining ingredients through funnel into bag.

NOTE: For 3½- to 4-pound turkey roast, bake in ungreased baking pan, 11 × 7 × 1½ inches, and double the amounts of remaining ingredients. Cut roast into ½-inch slices and spoon 1 tablespoon pan juice on each slice. (About 14 slices/95 calories each.)

A cup of this cut-up turkey without fatty skin comes to just 265 calories. Mix with Mock Mayonnaise (page 65) for a nice chunky salad—or slice the turkey for sandwiches.

TURKEY BURGERS

1 pound ground turkey	¼ cup jellied cranberry sauce
1 teaspoon salt	¼ teaspoon horseradish
¼ teaspoon sage	¼ cup water
2 tablespoons finely chopped onion	1 drop red food color (optional)

Use large skillet with non-stick finish or coat regular skillet with vegetable spray-on for cookware. Mix meat, salt, sage and onion. Shape mixture into 4 patties, about 3½ inches in diameter and ¾ inch thick. Cook in skillet over medium heat, turning frequently, until light brown and done, about 15 minutes.

While patties cook, heat remaining ingredients until hot, stirring occasionally. Spoon 2 tablespoons cranberry mixture onto each patty.

4 servings/255 calories each.

Turkey *and* cranberry sauce in unexpected burgers. Store ground turkey in the coldest part of the refrigerator and use within 24 hours, or freeze for future use.

TURKEY MEATBALL MANDARIN

1 pound ground turkey	½ teaspoon crushed gingerroot
1 teaspoon salt	or ¼ teaspoon ground ginger
1 teaspoon instant minced onion	1 package (7 ounces) frozen
¼ teaspoon garlic powder	Chinese pea pods
1 tablespoon chopped pimiento	1 teaspoon cornstarch
1 tablespoon soy sauce	1 tablespoon water
1 egg	2 cups Hot Cooked Rice (page 10)
4 cups water	Parsley
1 teaspoon salt	1 can (11 ounces) mandarin orange
2 tablespoons soy sauce	segments, drained

Mix meat, 1 teaspoon salt, the onion, garlic powder, pimiento, 1 tablespoon soy sauce and the egg thoroughly. Shape mixture into 1½-inch balls.

In large skillet, heat 4 cups water, 1 teaspoon salt, 2 tablespoons soy sauce and the gingerroot to boiling. Place meatballs in seasoned water; heat to boiling. Reduce heat; cover and simmer until meatballs are done, about 30 minutes. While meatballs simmer, cook pea pods as directed on package; drain.

With slotted spoon, remove meatballs to warm platter. Strain liquid; reserve 1 cup. Mix cornstarch and 1 tablespoon water in same skillet. Stir in reserved liquid. Cook, stirring constantly, until mixture thickens and boils. Boil and stir 1 minute.

Arrange meatballs on rice. Arrange pea pods around meatballs; garnish with parsley and orange segments. Serve with gravy.

6 servings/250 calories each. (Each serving: 3 meatballs, ½ cup rice, pea pods and orange segments, 2 tablespoons gravy.)

Variation

Beef Meatball Mandarin: Substitute 1 pound lean ground beef for the ground turkey; decrease salt in meat mixture to ¾ teaspoon. (6 servings/260 calories each. Each serving: 3 meatballs, ½ cup rice, pea pods and orange segments, 2 tablespoons gravy.)

Get into action. Set a time to exercise regularly—then make it a must till it turns into a habit.

CHICKEN WITH MUSHROOM GRAVY

6 chicken breast halves (3 pounds)
1 cup tomato juice
1 can (4 ounces) mushroom stems
   and pieces, drained (reserve
   liquid)
⅓ cup finely chopped onion

1 tablespoon parsley flakes
1½ teaspoons salt
1 teaspoon basil leaves
⅛ teaspoon garlic powder
2 teaspoons cornstarch
2 tablespoons water

Remove skin from chicken. Use large skillet with non-stick finish or coat regular skillet with vegetable spray-on for cookware. Heat skillet; brown chicken over medium-high heat. Pour tomato juice and reserved mushroom liquid onto chicken. Stir in onion, parsley flakes, salt, basil leaves and garlic powder. Cover and simmer until chicken is tender, 50 to 60 minutes. Stir in mushrooms.

Mix cornstarch and water; stir into liquid in skillet. Cook, stirring constantly, until mixture thickens and boils. Boil and stir 1 minute.

6 servings/230 calories each.

Double savings: Skinning the chicken subtracts 70 calories for three ounces of bird; non-stick, non-fat cooking saves more. Pictured on the cover.

PEPPER CHICKEN

2½- to 3-pound broiler-fryer
   chicken, cut up
¼ cup soy sauce
1 tablespoon water
½ teaspoon garlic powder
1 can (8½ ounces) water chestnuts,
   drained and sliced

1 green pepper, cut into 1-inch
   pieces
2 teaspoons cornstarch
2 tablespoons water

Remove skin and fat from chicken. Place chicken in large skillet. Mix soy sauce, 1 tablespoon water and the garlic powder; pour over chicken. Cover and refrigerate 1 hour, turning chicken once.

Heat to boiling; reduce heat and simmer 40 minutes. Scatter water chestnut slices and green pepper pieces on chicken; cover and simmer until chicken is tender, 15 to 20 minutes.

Mix cornstarch and 2 tablespoons water; stir into liquid in skillet. Cook, stirring constantly, until mixture thickens and boils. Boil and stir 1 minute.

6 servings/190 calories each.

Be a lean-meat cook. Trim fat before you bake, broil, roast or stew. Chill homemade stews and soups; skim fat from the top and discard, then reheat the mixture. Skin chicken and fish before cooking or before eating.

SAN FRANCISCO CHICKEN SALAD

3 chicken breast halves (about 1½ pounds)
½ teaspoon crushed gingerroot or ¼ teaspoon ground ginger
½ teaspoon salt
1 medium head lettuce

3 green onions, cut into 1½-inch strips
2 medium tomatoes, cut into thin wedges
¼ cup toasted sesame seed*
Oil-and-Vinegar Dressing (below)

Remove skin from chicken. Place chicken in large saucepan; add enough water to cover. Add gingerroot and salt; heat to boiling. Reduce heat; cover and simmer until chicken is tender, 30 to 40 minutes. Remove from heat; cool chicken in broth.

Remove meat from bones; cut meat into 1-inch pieces (about 3 cups). Into large bowl, tear lettuce into bite-size pieces. Add chicken, onions, tomatoes, sesame seed and dressing; toss.

6 servings/155 calories each. (Each serving: 1½ cups.)

Oil-and-Vinegar Dressing

1 tablespoon sugar
2 tablespoons vinegar
1 tablespoon salad oil

1½ teaspoons salt
1 teaspoon monosodium glutamate
½ teaspoon pepper

Shake all ingredients in tightly covered jar.

*To toast sesame seed, spread on ungreased baking sheet and bake in 350° oven, stirring occasionally, until golden, 10 to 15 minutes.

WINE JELLY

1 cup port
1 cup low-calorie strawberry-flavored soda pop (no sugar)

1 tablespoon sugar
1 envelope unflavored gelatin
1 to 2 drops red food color

Measure port, soda pop and sugar into small saucepan. Sprinkle gelatin on liquid to soften. Stir over low heat until gelatin is dissolved. Heat to boiling. Stir in food color. Immediately pour into two 1-cup jelly glasses. Cool. Cover and refrigerate until thickened. Refrigerate no longer than 3 weeks.

Two 1-cup glasses/10 calories per tablespoon.

Pictured on page 23:
385-Calorie Dinner—
Rosy Consommé (page 67),
San Francisco Chicken Salad (this page),
Broccoli Spears (¾ cup) with Butter (1 teaspoon),
Triangle Crackers,
Rocky Road Cheese Fruit Whip (page 59).

Total Calories 385

395 Calories

COMPANY FISH ROULADES

2 pounds frozen fish fillets
(skinless), thawed
2 tablespoons lemon juice
Paprika
Salt and pepper

About 8 large dill pickles, cut
crosswise into 1-inch pieces
16 lemon slices
⅓ cup chili sauce
2 packages (10 ounces each)
frozen chopped spinach

Heat oven to 350°. Cut fish fillets into strips 1 inch wide and long enough to wrap around pickle pieces. Sprinkle both sides of fish strips with lemon juice, paprika, salt and pepper. Roll a fish strip around each pickle piece; secure with wooden picks. Place fish rolls upright on ungreased rack in broiler pan. Top each with a lemon slice and 1 teaspoon chili sauce. Bake until fish flakes easily with a fork, 20 to 25 minutes.

While fish roulades are baking, cook spinach as directed on package; drain. Turn into serving dish; place hot fish roulades on top.

8 servings/155 calories each. (Each serving: 2 roulades, about ⅓ cup spinach.)

BAKED FLOUNDER VINAIGRETTE

2 packages (16 ounces each)
frozen flounder fillets (skinless)
Paprika
Salt
Six 1½-inch-thick tomato slices

1 tablespoon snipped chives
½ teaspoon tarragon leaves
½ cup low-calorie Italian dressing
¼ cup shredded Cheddar cheese
1 tablespoon snipped parsley

Heat oven to 475°. Use baking pan, 13 × 9 × 2 inches, with non-stick finish or coat regular baking pan with vegetable spray-on for cookware. Cut each frozen block of fish into 3 pieces. (Let fish stand at room temperature 10 minutes before cutting.)

Arrange fish in baking pan. Sprinkle with paprika and salt. Place a tomato slice on each serving; sprinkle with salt, chives and tarragon leaves. Pour dressing on fish and top each serving with 2 teaspoons cheese. Bake uncovered until fish flakes easily with a fork, 20 to 25 minutes. Sprinkle parsley on each serving.

6 servings/145 calories each.

Poke a hole in the end of a lemon with a wooden pick—now you have a super squirter for fish, salads or vegetables.

Pictured on page 24:
395-Calorie Dinner—
Company Fish Roulades
(this page),
Sea Breeze Tossed Potato
Salad (page 32),
Carrot Sticks,
Lacy Melba Toast (page 64),
Melon (⅛) with Grapes
(⅓ cup),
Skim Milk (1 cup).

DILLED FISH STICKS

1 package (16 ounces) frozen pike or flounder fillets (skinless)
1 teaspoon salt
½ teaspoon dill weed
2 drops red pepper sauce
⅓ cup unsweetened grapefruit juice

½ teaspoon paprika
2 teaspoons finely chopped onion
Six ¼-inch-thick lengthwise slices dill pickle
Sprigs of dill or parsley

Cut frozen block of fish into 6 sticks. (To make this easier, let fish stand at room temperature 10 minutes before cutting.)

Arrange fish in ungreased baking pan, 13 × 9 × 2 inches. Mix salt, dill weed, red pepper sauce and grapefruit juice; pour over fish. Let stand at room temperature 1 hour, turning fish frequently.

Heat oven to 475°. Sprinkle fish with paprika, then top each piece with onion and a dill pickle slice. Bake uncovered until fish flakes easily with a fork, about 15 minutes. Garnish with sprigs of dill.

3 servings/120 calories each. (Each serving: 2 sticks.)

FAST FISH CHOWDER

1 pound fresh or frozen pike, pollock or halibut fillets
3 cups tomato juice
1 medium onion, sliced
3 lemon slices

1 bay leaf
½ teaspoon salt
2 peppercorns
Snipped parsley

Thaw fish if frozen. Cut fish into bite-size pieces. In large saucepan, heat remaining ingredients except parsley to boiling. Add fish; heat to boiling. Reduce heat; cover and simmer until fish flakes easily with a fork, 4 to 6 minutes. Serve in soup bowls and sprinkle each serving with parsley.

5 servings/125 calories each. (Each serving: 1 cup.)

Sobering thought: One hundred extra calories a day— 1 tablespoon of butter or a 2-inch biscuit or a scoop of ice milk—can add up to 10 extra pounds in a year.

PARTY SHRIMP ORIENTAL

1 **pound cleaned raw shrimp, fresh or frozen (about 2 cups)**
2 **tablespoons soy sauce**
1 **tablespoon sherry**
1 **teaspoon crushed gingerroot or ½ teaspoon ground ginger**
¼ **teaspoon salt**
1½ **cups sliced onion**
1 **cup ¼-inch diagonal slices celery**

1 **can (8½ ounces) water chestnuts, drained and sliced**
1 **can (16 ounces) bean sprouts, rinsed and drained**
1 **tablespoon cornstarch**
½ **teaspoon instant chicken bouillon**
½ **cup water**
6 **slices Lacy Melba Toast (page 64)**

Dish up servings in the kitchen instead of from platters and vegetable dishes at the table. That way you can give yourself exact measured amounts. (Handy device: a #8 ice-cream scoop measures ½ cup— of anything.)

In large skillet, cook and stir shrimp, soy sauce, sherry, gingerroot and salt over high heat until shrimp are pink, about 6 minutes. Remove shrimp and set aside.

In same skillet, cook and stir onion, celery, water chestnuts and bean sprouts until celery is crisp-tender, about 6 minutes. Stir in shrimp. Mix cornstarch, bouillon and water. Stir into shrimp mixture. Cook, stirring constantly, until mixture thickens and boils. Boil and stir 1 minute. Serve shrimp mixture over toast.

6 servings / 165 calories each. (Each serving: scant 1 cup shrimp mixture, 1 slice toast.)

BROILED SOY HALIBUT STEAKS

2 **pounds halibut steaks (about 6)**
3 **tablespoons soy sauce**
1 **teaspoon ginger**
½ **teaspoon garlic powder**
1 **teaspoon grated lemon peel**

¼ **cup lemon juice**
¼ **cup water**
Lemon slices
Parsley

Crusty and flaky, with an elusive whisper of garlic. This recipe's just as good with salmon.

Place fish in ungreased baking dish, 13½ × 9 × 2 inches. Mix remaining ingredients except lemon slices and parsley; pour onto fish. Cover and refrigerate at least 8 hours.

Set oven control at broil and/or 550°. Drain fish; reserve marinade. Place fish on greased rack in broiler pan. Brushing fish occasionally with reserved marinade, broil with top 4 inches from heat 5 to 7 minutes on each side. Garnish with lemon slices and parsley.

6 servings / 160 calories each.

SALMON-CITRUS SALAD

1 carton (8 ounces) unflavored yogurt (1 cup)	1 can (16 ounces) salmon, cleaned, drained and broken into pieces
1 tablespoon grated grapefruit peel	1 grapefruit, pared and sectioned
½ teaspoon salt	1 teaspoon seasoned salt
3 cups bite-size pieces spinach (about 3 ounces)	1 tablespoon tarragon vinegar
1 cup thin diagonal slices celery	Romaine leaves
	Paprika

Mix yogurt, grapefruit peel and salt in small bowl; cover and refrigerate until serving time.

Toss remaining ingredients except romaine leaves and paprika. Turn salad into bowl lined with romaine leaves; sprinkle with paprika. Serve with yogurt dressing.

6 servings / 145 calories each. (Each serving: 1 cup.)

TUNA PINEAPPLE BOATS

1 pineapple	¼ teaspoon ginger
2 cans (7 ounces each) white tuna in water, drained and broken into chunks	2 tablespoons lime juice
	2 tablespoons coarsely chopped dry roasted almonds
1 cup strawberries (reserve 4 whole berries for garnish), sliced	Dash ginger
2 cups cantaloupe or honeydew melon balls	Pineapple yogurt

Select a pineapple with fresh green leaves. Cut pineapple lengthwise into quarters through green top. Cut along curved edges of quarters with grapefruit knife to remove fruit. Cut fruit into chunks; remove core. Drain fruit and invert shells to drain.

Place pineapple chunks, tuna, sliced strawberries and melon balls in large bowl. Sprinkle with ¼ teaspoon ginger and the lime juice and toss. Cover and refrigerate 1 hour.

Spoon pineapple mixture into shells; sprinkle with almonds and dash ginger. Spoon 1 tablespoon yogurt onto each serving and garnish with reserved whole strawberries.

4 servings / 255 calories each.

Don't let a lapse throw you. If you do go over your calorie count, resolve to start over at the next meal. Think success!

OVEN OMELET WITH SPINACH

1 package (10 ounces) frozen chopped spinach	1 teaspoon salt
9 eggs	½ teaspoon basil leaves
2 tablespoons instant minced onion	¼ teaspoon garlic powder
2 tablespoons skim milk	8 peeled tomato slices
	½ cup shredded mozzarella cheese

Heat oven to 325°. Use baking pan, 11 × 7 × 1½ inches, with non-stick finish or coat regular pan with vegetable spray-on for cookware. Cook spinach as directed on package; drain.

Beat eggs until light and fluffy. Stir in spinach, onion, skim milk, salt, basil leaves and garlic powder. Pour into pan. Arrange tomato slices on top and sprinkle with cheese. Bake uncovered until set, 25 to 30 minutes.

8 servings/135 calories each.

Fluffy main-dish delight. Golden brown with cheese and tomatoes on top, it's a satisfying supper. Serve with Tangy Mushroom Salad (page 31), fresh fruit, and that's it.

QUICHE FRANCAISE

1½ cups hot cooked regular rice	¼ teaspoon salt
1 tablespoon snipped chives	½ cup shredded mozzarella or Monterey (Jack) cheese
1 egg white	2 tablespoons instant minced onion
1 package (3 ounces) sliced smoked beef	8 tomato slices
3 eggs plus 1 egg yolk	
1 can (13 ounces) evaporated skim milk	

Heat oven to 350°. Use 10-inch pie pan with non-stick finish or coat regular pie pan with vegetable spray-on for cookware. Beat rice, chives and egg white with fork. Turn mixture into pie pan; spread evenly with rubber scraper on bottom and halfway up side of pie pan. (Do not leave any holes.) Bake 5 minutes.

Tear meat into small pieces and sprinkle in rice crust. Beat eggs, egg yolk, skim milk and salt thoroughly; stir in cheese and onion. Carefully pour into rice crust. Bake until knife inserted 1 inch from edge comes out clean, 25 to 30 minutes. Immediately run knife around edge to loosen crust. Let quiche stand 10 minutes before serving. Cut into wedges; top each wedge with a tomato slice.

8 servings/190 calories each.

Food for thought: If this quiche were baked in a pie shell, it would cost upwards of a thousand calories more. The rice crust saves about 145 calories a serving.

CHINESE QUICHE

1 cup hot cooked regular rice
1 teaspoon soy sauce
¼ teaspoon ginger
1 egg white
2 eggs plus 1 egg yolk
1 cup skim milk
¾ teaspoon salt

½ can (16-ounce size) Chinese vegetables, drained (1 cup)
1 cup cut-up cooked chicken
2 green onions, sliced (with tops)
Pimiento strips
Spicy Soy Sauce (below)

Heat oven to 350°. Use 9-inch pie pan with non-stick finish or coat regular pie pan with vegetable spray-on for cookware. Beat rice, soy sauce, ginger and egg white with fork. Turn mixture into pie pan; spread evenly with rubber scraper on bottom and halfway up side of pie pan. (Do not leave any holes.)

Beat eggs, egg yolk, milk and salt thoroughly; stir in vegetables, chicken and onions. Carefully pour into rice crust. Bake until knife inserted 1 inch from edge comes out clean, 30 to 40 minutes. Immediately run knife around edge to loosen crust. Let quiche stand 10 minutes before serving. Cut into wedges; garnish with pimiento strips and serve with Spicy Soy Sauce.

8 servings / 135 calories each.

Spicy Soy Sauce
Mix 3 tablespoons soy sauce, ½ cup water and ⅛ teaspoon ginger.

BAKED EGG WITH BROCCOLI

Heat oven to 325°. For each serving, coat a 6-ounce custard cup with vegetable spray-on for cookware. Place 2 tablespoons cooked chopped broccoli in cup; season with garlic salt. Carefully break an egg into cup; season with salt. Sprinkle 1 tablespoon shredded Cheddar cheese on top of egg. Bake uncovered until egg is desired consistency, 15 to 18 minutes. Serve in custard cup or unmold onto serving plate.

1 serving / 110 calories.

Be a con artist. Arrange foods attractively to fill your plate. Use smaller-size dishes, spread food out and conceal any gaps with vegetable snacks (page 37), celery leaves or parsley.

TANGY MUSHROOM SALAD

For each serving, tear Bibb or Boston lettuce into bite-size pieces (¾ cup) into salad bowl. Add ¼ cup sliced fresh mushrooms and 1 tablespoon Make-your-own Cocktail Sauce (below) and toss.

1 serving/35 calories.

Make-your-own Cocktail Sauce

1 bottle (12 ounces) chili sauce	½ teaspoon Worcestershire sauce
1 tablespoon horseradish	¼ teaspoon salt
1 tablespoon lemon juice	Dash pepper

Mix all ingredients. Refrigerate leftover sauce. (About 1½ cups/15 calories per tablespoon.)

Variation

Tangy Shrimp Appetizer Salad: Add ¼ cup cleaned cooked shrimp with the mushrooms. (1 serving/75 calories.)

SPINACH-SPROUT SALAD

8 ounces spinach or curly endive	Sesame Dressing (below)
1 can (16 ounces) bean sprouts, rinsed and drained	1 cup croutons (optional)
1 can (8½ ounces) water chestnuts, drained and sliced	

Tear spinach into bite-size pieces into salad bowl. Add bean sprouts, water chestnuts and dressing and toss. Sprinkle croutons on top.

8 servings/25 calories each without croutons; 65 calories each with croutons. (Each serving: ¾ cup.)

Sesame Dressing

¼ cup soy sauce	1 tablespoon finely chopped onion
2 tablespoons toasted sesame seed*	½ teaspoon sugar
2 tablespoons lemon juice	¼ teaspoon pepper

Mix all ingredients.

* To toast sesame seed, spread on ungreased baking sheet and bake in 350° oven, stirring occasionally, until golden, 10 to 15 minutes.

Salads and Vegetables— Your Biggest Breaks

or

How to Fill Up with Fewer Calories

Greens are great—colorful, crisp and practically scot-free of calories. To add zip to them, toss in crunchy raw vegetables or naturally sweet, tangy fruits and low-calorie dressings. Along with salads, serve cooked vegetables— hot, filling and superbly seasoned with herbs and spices instead of butter and rich sauces. Together, salads and vegetables make up a very important part of your nutritional needs. And you get so much for the calories spent!

SEA BREEZE TOSSED POTATO SALAD

A real potato-lover's calorie bargain. In a hurry? Use little canned potatoes. Pictured on page 24.

½ cup low-calorie Italian dressing
2 cups hot cubed cooked potatoes
1 small cucumber
4 hard-cooked eggs, each cut into
  4 wedges
1 cup ½-inch diagonal slices
  celery
½ teaspoon seasoned salt
1 tablespoon dill weed
3 cups bite-size pieces lettuce
2 tablespoons snipped parsley

Pour dressing over potatoes in large bowl; cover and refrigerate 1 hour.

Thinly slice unpared cucumber into bowl; add remaining ingredients except parsley and toss. Sprinkle parsley on top.

8 servings/75 calories each. (Each serving: ¾ cup.)

TOSSED SALAD ITALIANO

For a fancier presentation, line a platter with greens, arrange the vegetables separately on it, put dressing in a cruet. Presto! A colorful salad buffet.

1 package (9 ounces) frozen
  Italian green beans, cooked,
  drained and cooled
1 pound small zucchini (about 4),
  cut into ¼-inch slices
1 small onion, thinly sliced
1 cup cherry tomatoes, cut into
  halves
¼ teaspoon garlic salt
½ cup low-calorie Italian dressing
2 tablespoons shredded mozzarella
  cheese

Combine vegetables in bowl and sprinkle with garlic salt. Pour dressing over vegetables and toss. Sprinkle cheese on top.

6 servings/50 calories each. (Each serving: ⅔ cup.)

WINTER TOMATO SALAD

1 small cauliflower, separated
  into flowerets
1 can (16 ounces) tomato
  wedges, drained
½ cup chopped onion
1 tablespoon vinegar
1 teaspoon seasoned salt
¼ teaspoon pepper
6 lettuce cups

Toss all ingredients except lettuce cups in bowl. Cover and refrigerate at least 30 minutes.

With slotted spoon, remove vegetables to lettuce cups.

6 servings/35 calories each. (Each serving: ¾ cup.)

GAZPACHO MOLD

2 cups vegetable juice cocktail
2 teaspoons instant beef bouillon
2 envelopes unflavored gelatin
2 to 3 tablespoons wine vinegar
2 tomatoes, peeled and coarsely
   chopped

1 small cucumber, cut into ¼-
   inch cubes
2 teaspoons instant minced onion
¾ teaspoon salt
6 drops red pepper sauce
Leaf lettuce

Sophisticated Mexican cold soup turned into a molded salad. Recommended for adult tastes only.

Combine vegetable juice cocktail and bouillon in medium saucepan. Sprinkle gelatin on liquid to soften. Stir over medium heat until gelatin is dissolved, about 3 minutes. Stir in vinegar. Refrigerate until slightly thickened but not set.

Stir in tomatoes, cucumber, onion, salt and red pepper sauce. Pour into baking pan, 8 × 8 × 2 inches, or 5-cup ring mold. Refrigerate until set, about 4 hours. Unmold onto lettuce.

9 servings/30 calories each. (Each serving: about ¾ cup.)

CONSOMME VEGETABLE WREATH

1 can (10½ ounces) condensed
   consommé (beef gelatin added)
1 cup water
¼ teaspoon garlic salt
1 tablespoon Worcestershire sauce

1 envelope unflavored gelatin
1 cup uncooked cauliflowerets
1 cup small cherry tomatoes
Yogurt Dressing (below)

True party fare, an eye-catcher on a buffet with ham or beef. And only you will guess that a generous serving, complete with dressing, is a mere 40 calories.

Combine consommé, water, garlic salt and Worcestershire sauce in small saucepan. Sprinkle gelatin on liquid to soften. Stir over medium heat until gelatin is dissolved, about 3 minutes. Refrigerate until slightly thickened but not set.

Pour about ⅓ of gelatin mixture into 5-cup ring mold. Arrange vegetables in gelatin. Pour remaining gelatin mixture on vegetables. Refrigerate until set, about 4 hours.

Unmold onto serving plate. Cut into 6 servings. Spoon 2 tablespoons Yogurt Dressing on each serving.

6 servings/40 calories each. (Each serving: ¾ cup.)

Yogurt Dressing

Mix 1 carton (8 ounces) unflavored yogurt (1 cup), 1 teaspoon horseradish, ½ teaspoon salt and ¼ teaspoon garlic salt.

CANTALOUPE MOLD WITH TEAHOUSE TOPPING

Pictured on page 38.

1 cup boiling water
1 envelope low-calorie orange-
   flavored gelatin
¾ cup unsweetened orange juice

¼ teaspoon ginger
2 cups small melon balls (cantaloupe and/or honeydew)
Teahouse Topping (below)

Pour boiling water on gelatin in bowl; stir until gelatin is dissolved. Stir in orange juice and ginger. Refrigerate until slightly thickened but not set.

Stir in melon balls. Pour into a 4-cup mold or 6 individual molds. Refrigerate until set, about 4 hours. Unmold onto serving plate. Spoon 1 generous tablespoon Teahouse Topping onto each serving.

6 servings/60 calories each. (Each serving: ⅔ cup.)

Teahouse Topping

Mix ½ cup frozen whipped topping (thawed) and 1 teaspoon instant tea.

MEXICAN SALAD

About dressing. Our salad recipes call for specific amounts of dressing; they're included in the calorie count for the salad. To help you figure extra-helping costs, calories are given for individual dressings.

1 small head lettuce
2 large oranges, pared and
   sectioned, or 1 can (11 ounces)
   mandarin orange segments, drained
1 cucumber, scored and sliced
1 small onion, thinly sliced
   and separated into rings

2 tablespoons chopped red
   chilies or pimiento
½ teaspoon chili powder
Chili Dressing (below)

Coarsely shred lettuce. Toss lettuce and remaining ingredients except Chili Dressing in bowl. Spoon 1 tablespoon dressing onto each serving.

8 servings/40 calories each. (Each serving: ¾ cup.)

Chili Dressing

Mix 1 carton (8 ounces) unflavored yogurt (1 cup), 1 tablespoon chili sauce and 1 teaspoon onion salt. (1 cup/10 calories per tablespoon.)

PICKLED ARTICHOKES

1 can (14 ounces) artichoke hearts,
    drained (reserve liquid)
2 tablespoons instant minced onion
3 tablespoons dry sherry (optional)

2 tablespoons soy sauce
¼ cup vinegar
1 teaspoon salt

Place artichokes in 1-quart standard jar. Heat reserved artichoke liquid and remaining ingredients to boiling; pour into jar. Cover and refrigerate 24 hours. Drain; serve artichokes in salad or as a relish.

4 servings/30 calories each without sherry; 45 calories each with sherry. (Each serving: ½ cup.)

PICKLED MUSHROOMS

36 small mushroom caps or 16
    large mushrooms, cut into halves
¼ cup vinegar
3 tablespoons dry sherry (optional)

2 tablespoons soy sauce
1 teaspoon salt
½ small onion, sliced and
    separated into rings

Place mushrooms in 1-quart standard jar. Heat remaining ingredients to boiling; pour into jar. Cover and refrigerate at least 24 hours. Drain; serve mushrooms and onions in salad or as a relish.

4 servings/40 calories each without sherry; 55 calories each with sherry. (Each serving: ½ cup.)

PICKLED CUCUMBERS

1 cucumber
½ medium onion, thinly sliced
    and separated into rings
½ cup vinegar

½ cup water
¼ teaspoon salt
Dash pepper

Run tines of fork lengthwise on unpared cucumber. Thinly slice cucumber into bowl. Add onion rings. Mix remaining ingredients; pour onto vegetables. Cover and refrigerate at least 1 hour. Drain before serving.

4 servings/15 calories each. (Each serving: about ½ cup.)

When you get hungry (and you will), don't panic. Fill up on snacks (see some examples on page 37), or lose yourself in a "hungry job"— clean a drawer, weed the garden, give yourself a facial.

Take a reading on all the low-calorie salad dressings that now come bottled. And while you're at it, compare the counts—they vary quite a bit. Or try Mock Mayonnaise (page 65). The Fluffy Fruit Dressing is pictured on the cover.

Pictured on page 37:
Snacks—
For specific calories for items or groups of items pictured, see pages 72-74.

Pictured on page 38:
405-Calorie Dinner—
Pork Tenderloin Chow Mein (page 17),
Cantaloupe Mold with Teahouse Topping (page 34),
Rice (⅓ cup),
Homemade Lime Sherbet (page 49).

SALAD DRESSINGS

Cucumber Dressing

½ cup chopped cucumber
1½ teaspoons instant minced onion
1 teaspoon horseradish
½ teaspoon salt
1 carton (8 ounces) unflavored yogurt (1 cup)

Beat all ingredients with rotary beater. Refrigerate leftover dressing.

1¼ cups / 10 calories per tablespoon.

Curry-Caper Dressing or Dip

1 carton (8 ounces) unflavored yogurt (1 cup)
¼ cup mayonnaise or salad dressing
¼ teaspoon salt
¼ teaspoon curry powder
⅛ teaspoon garlic powder
½ teaspoon instant beef bouillon
2 tablespoons capers, drained

Measure all ingredients into blender. Cover and blend on medium speed 10 seconds. Scrape sides with rubber spatula; blend 10 seconds longer. Refrigerate leftover dressing.

2½ cups / 20 calories per tablespoon.

Creamy Orange Dressing

Shake 1 can (13 ounces) evaporated skim milk and 1 can (6 ounces) frozen orange juice concentrate (thawed) in tightly covered jar. Refrigerate leftover dressing.

2 cups / 20 calories per tablespoon.

Fluffy Fruit Dressing

Beat 1 carton (8 ounces) unflavored yogurt (1 cup) and 3 tablespoons raspberry or strawberry jam or orange marmalade with rotary beater. Refrigerate leftover dressing.

1 cup / 20 calories per tablespoon.

70-80 CALORIES EACH

20-30 CALORIES EACH

50-60 CALORIES EACH

NO COUNT

4
lunches under
300
calories

FOUR LUNCHES UNDER 300 CALORIES

Spring Fever Soup 'n Sandwich/280 calories
Quick Spinach Soup (page 67), Open-face Chicken Sandwich (page 65), Strawberries (½ cup), Sugar (2 teaspoons), Skim Milk (1 cup).

Summer Fruit 'n Ham Plate/280 calories
Lean Ham Slices (2 ounces) on Leaf Lettuce, Cantaloupe (¼ melon, 5 inches in diameter) with Blueberries (½ cup), Lacy Melba Toast (page 64), Neufchâtel Cheese (½ ounce), Iced Tea.

Autumn Broiler Lunch/295 calories
Bean Sprout Burger (page 11), Thin Toasted Bun Slice (¼ bun), Versatile Mushroom Topper (this page), Broccoli Flowerets, Broiled Tomato Half, Celery Stalk, Root Beer in the Clouds (page 62).

Winter Salad-Sandwich Plate/250 calories
Tangy Shrimp Appetizer Salad (page 31), Crunchy Cottage Cheese (page 65) on Rye, Beans (½ cup), Carrots, Olives, Broiled Grapefruit.

EASY BAKED ASPARAGUS

Heat oven to 325°. Break off tough ends of 1 pound asparagus as far down as stalks snap easily. Place stalks in single layer in ungreased baking pan, 8 × 8 × 2 inches. Sprinkle with ½ teaspoon seasoned salt, ½ teaspoon salt and 1 tablespoon water. Cover tightly with aluminum foil and bake until tender, 20 to 30 minutes.

4 servings/30 calories each.

VERSATILE MUSHROOM TOPPER

Cook and stir ½ pound mushrooms (if they are large, cut into slices), 1 teaspoon water and 1 teaspoon instant beef bouillon in skillet over medium heat until bouillon is dissolved and mushrooms are hot.

4 servings/20 calories each. (Each serving: ¼ cup.)

When you're lunching solo: Sit down. Eat slowly. After every third bite put your fork down and pause. You'll find that the more time you take to eat, the less food it takes to satisfy you.

Pictured on page 39:
395-Calorie Dinner—
No-Noodle Lasagne (page 14), Orange-Onion Salad (¾ cup) with Cucumber Dressing (page 36, 1 tablespoon), Bread Stick (4-inch), Frosty Eggnog (page 57).

Pictured on page 40:
Four Lunches Under 300 Calories (this page).

ITALIAN CABBAGE WEDGES

Bulky foods that fill you up: a mound of green vegetables, a giant salad with low-calorie dressing or a big bowl of ready-to-eat unsweetened cereal.

Cut 2-pound cabbage into 6 wedges; remove core. In large skillet, heat 1 inch salted water (½ teaspoon salt to 1 cup water) to boiling. Add cabbage; cover and heat to boiling. Cook until crisp-tender, 10 to 12 minutes; drain.

Place cabbage on serving platter. Cut three 1-ounce slices mozzarella cheese in half. Place half-slice cheese on each cabbage wedge. Garnish each with strip of pimiento and sprinkle with oregano leaves.

6 servings/75 calories each.

JAPANESE-STYLE CABBAGE

Actual cooking for this recipe takes just about five minutes. You can chop the cabbage ahead of time, and while you're at it, chop some extra and snack on it freely—only 20 calories for a whole cup.

½ cup chicken broth	1 cup sliced celery
2 tablespoons soy sauce	1 tablespoon chopped green onion
4 cups thinly sliced cabbage	

In large skillet, heat chicken broth and soy sauce to boiling. Stir in cabbage, celery and onion. Cook over high heat, turning vegetables frequently with pancake turner, until crisp-tender, about 5 minutes. Do not overcook.

4 servings/30 calories each. (Each serving: about ½ cup.)

IRISH MASHED POTATOES

Cabbage makes potatoes go further with fewer calories—perks up the texture, too!

2 cups shredded green cabbage (about ½ small)	¼ cup sliced green onion
Instant mashed potato puffs (enough for 4 servings)	Dash pepper

Heat ½ inch salted water (½ teaspoon salt to 1 cup water) to boiling. Add cabbage; cover and heat to boiling. Cook 5 minutes; drain.

Prepare instant mashed potato puffs as directed on package except—increase salt to ¾ teaspoon, omit butter and substitute skim milk for the milk. Fold in onion, pepper and hot cabbage.

6 servings/55 calories each. (Each serving: ⅔ cup.)

CELERY POLYNESIAN

1 teaspoon salad oil	1 tablespoon instant chicken bouillon
5 cups ¼-inch diagonal slices celery	½ teaspoon salt
	½ teaspoon celery salt
1 can (8½ ounces) water chestnuts, drained and sliced	1 jar (2 ounces) sliced pimiento, drained

Heat oil in large skillet. Cook celery, water chestnuts, bouillon and seasonings in oil over medium heat, turning vegetables constantly with pancake turner, until celery is crisp-tender, about 10 minutes. Stir in pimiento and heat.

5 servings/45 calories each. (Each serving: 1 cup.)

SPINACH CONTINENTAL

2 packages (10 ounces each) frozen chopped spinach	2 teaspoons instant minced onion
	1½ teaspoons salt
1 can (4 ounces) mushroom stems and pieces, drained (reserve liquid)	¼ teaspoon garlic powder
	1 carton (8 ounces) unflavored yogurt (1 cup)
1 can (8½ ounces) water chestnuts, drained and sliced	

Cook spinach as directed on package except—use reserved mushroom liquid and enough water (not salted) to measure ½ cup; drain. Stir in remaining ingredients. Heat over low heat, stirring occasionally, just until mixture simmers.

6 servings/80 calories each. (Each serving: ⅔ cup.)

SOUTHERN RICE AND TOMATOES WITH ARTICHOKES

1 can (14 ounces) artichoke hearts	1 tablespoon dried shredded green onion or 3 green onions, cut up
1 can (16 ounces) stewed tomatoes	
1½ cups uncooked instant rice	¼ teaspoon salt

In large skillet, heat artichoke hearts (with liquid), tomatoes, rice, onion and salt to boiling, stirring frequently. Reduce heat; cover and simmer until rice is tender, about 10 minutes.

8 servings/100 calories each. (Each serving: ⅔ cup.)

Get back to nature. Learn to enjoy the built-in flavor of vegetables without butter, sauce or too much salt. Example: How long has it been since you washed and ate a tomato, right off the vine and seasoned with nothing but sunshine?

SEASONED MIXED VEGETABLES

Some fresh, some frozen, all seasoned and cooked together in the same pan.

2 cups water
1 envelope (.77 ounce) bacon-flavored salad dressing mix
1 cup ¼-inch-thick carrot sticks
1 package (10 ounces) frozen cauliflower

1 package (6 ounces) frozen Chinese pea pods
1 cup mushrooms, trimmed
4 lettuce cups

Heat water and salad dressing mix in large saucepan to boiling, stirring occasionally. Add carrot sticks; heat to boiling. Cover and boil 2 minutes. Add frozen vegetables; heat to boiling. Cover and boil 2 minutes. Stir in mushrooms; remove from heat. Cool vegetables in liquid. Refrigerate about 3 hours. With slotted spoon, remove vegetables to lettuce cups.

4 servings / 65 calories each. (Each serving: ¾ cup.)

EASY BROILED ZUCCHINI

Nice little slices of garlic-flavored squash. At 25 calories a serving, you can even afford to splurge with a sprinkle of grated cheese (30 calories a tablespoon). And it's so easy to stretch this recipe—simply add another squash or two. Pictured on the cover.

Cut 4 small zucchini lengthwise in half. Set oven control at broil and/or 550°. Place slices cut sides up in broiler pan. Brush with salad oil and sprinkle with salt, garlic salt and pepper. Broil 3 inches from heat until tender, 6 to 10 minutes.

4 servings / 25 calories each.

CONVERTIBLE POTATO TOPPER AND DIP

¼ cup skim milk
2 cups 2% cottage cheese (small curd)

1 envelope (about 1½ ounces) onion soup mix

Place all ingredients in blender. Cover and blend on high speed until smooth and creamy. Cover and refrigerate at least 1 hour.

2 cups / 15 calories per tablespoon.

ROSY PEACHES FLAMBE

Evaporated Milk Whip (below) or
   Dry Milk Whip (page 62)
¼ cup currant jelly
½ cup low-calorie strawberry-
   flavored soda pop (no sugar)

4 large peaches, peeled and sliced
1 teaspoon lemon juice
¼ cup brandy

Prepare whip as directed except—turn whip into refrigerator tray and freeze at least 8 hours.

Heat jelly and soda pop in saucepan or chafing dish, stirring constantly, until jelly is melted and mixture is smooth. Stir in peach slices; cook over low heat until peaches are almost tender, about 3 minutes. Stir in lemon juice.

Cut frozen whip into 6 servings and place in dessert dishes. Heat brandy in long-handled ladle or small saucepan but do not boil. Ignite and pour over hot peach mixture. Stir sauce and peaches and spoon onto frozen whip.

6 servings/75 calories each.

Evaporated Milk Whip

⅓ cup evaporated skim milk
½ teaspoon unflavored gelatin
1 tablespoon water

2 tablespoons sugar
½ teaspoon vanilla

Pour milk into small mixer bowl; place in freezer until crystals form around edge, about 30 minutes.

Sprinkle gelatin on water to soften. Place over boiling water until gelatin is dissolved. Add sugar and vanilla to milk; beat on high speed until very thick and fluffy. Gradually beat in gelatin until mixture is very stiff. Serve immediately. (Or whip can be refrigerated up to 1 hour or frozen for making Root Beer in the Clouds [page 62] or Rosy Peaches Flambé [above].)

2 cups/5 calories per tablespoon.

Desserts—Pure Pleasure at Little "Price"

or

Any Day Can Have a Happy Ending

Fun. That's what desserts are. And lack of them can cause even the most dedicated calorie-counter to feel downhearted. Pangs of desire for a sweet may even scuttle the plans of the most earnest calorie-counter. To the rescue! The desserts in this chapter are the soul of sweet reasonableness—calorically speaking. Some are "extras," to eat after other nutritional needs have been met; others incorporate basic nutrients so artfully you'd never guess they were good for you. All, however, are calorie-cut to give you a treat without unbalancing your calorie budget.

MIX AND MATCH YOUR OWN LOW-CALORIE DESSERT

Surprise! Dessert can be a calorie bargain. For instance, for 85 calories you can have ½ cup strawberries, 1 tablespoon Neufchâtel cheese spread and 2 triangle crackers.

Fruit	Calories	Fruit	Calories
1 plum (2-inch)	25	¼ honeydew melon (5-inch diameter)	35
½ cup grapes	35	1 medium peach	35
⅓ cup blueberries	30	1 medium apple	90
½ cup strawberries	30	1 medium orange	75
¼ cup dark sweet cherries	35	1 medium pear	100
¼ cantaloupe (5-inch diameter)	30		

Cheese Spreads	Calories	Crackers	Calories
1 tablespoon (½ ounce) pasteurized Neufchâtel cheese spread* with		1 pretzel stick	5
		1 pizza-flavored rye wafer	20
Onion	35	Melba toast round (garlic, rye, white)	10
Pimientos	35	Triangle cracker	10
Clams	35	Chicken-flavored cracker	10
Bacon and horseradish	40	Ham-flavored cracker	10
Blue cheese	40	Barbecue-flavored cracker	15
Bacon	40	Shredded wheat wafer	20

*In 5-ounce jar.

FRUIT-CHEESE BUFFET

1 pound seedless green grapes, separated into small clusters
1 cantaloupe, pared and cut into thin wedges
⅛ watermelon (3 to 4 pounds), pared and cut into 2-inch pieces
1 pineapple, cut into rings, pared and cored

4 ounces mozzarella cheese, cut into 8 pieces
7-ounce Gouda cheese, cut into 14 wedges (casing left on)
½ pound dark sweet cherries
Lemon leaves

If you like, use the jewel-colored fruits as a center-piece, add cheese at dessert time. Pictured on page 53.

Mound grapes in center of large tray or serving plate. Arrange cantaloupe wedges and watermelon pieces alternately around grapes, then place pineapple rings and cheeses on plate. Garnish plate with cherries and lemon leaves.

About 10 servings/105 or 110 calories each. (Each serving: ½ cup fruit—65 calories; ½ ounce mozzarella cheese—40 calories, *or* 1 wedge (½ ounce) Gouda cheese—45 calories.)

PINK PEARS

4 pears, halved, pared and cored
1 can (12 ounces) low-calorie raspberry-flavored soda pop (no sugar), chilled

1 teaspoon cornstarch
1 tablespoon water
1 envelope (about 2 ounces) dessert topping mix

Sweets without sugar. Cut calories (lots of them!) with naturally sweet fruits—fresh, water-packed, canned in natural juices—and berries frozen unsweetened.

Place pear halves cut sides down in large skillet. Add 1 cup of the soda pop; cover and simmer until pears are tender, 8 to 10 minutes. Place a pear half cut side up in each dessert dish.

Mix cornstarch and water; stir into liquid in skillet. Cook, stirring constantly, until mixture thickens and boils. Boil and stir 1 minute. Pour onto pear halves.

Prepare topping mix as directed on package except—substitute remaining soda pop (½ cup) for the milk. Spoon 1 tablespoon topping onto each serving.

8 servings/65 calories each.

WATERMELON FRUIT BOWL

Spectacular showpiece for an outdoor buffet. A calorie-counter's bargain with or without wine.

Cut off lengthwise top third of large oblong watermelon, making a saw-toothed edge with sharp thin knife; cover and refrigerate top third for future use. Cut watermelon balls from larger section and refrigerate. Cut out remaining fruit, leaving a neat shell. Drain shell; cover and refrigerate.

At serving time, fill shell with watermelon balls, cantaloupe balls, pineapple chunks, banana slices, peach slices, strawberries, raspberries and blueberries or other fruits. Large shell will hold about 22 cups fruit. Drizzle 2 cans (6 ounces each) frozen pink lemonade concentrate (thawed) or 1½ cups dry sherry or rosé on fruit.

About 22 servings/70 to 85 calories each. (Each serving: 1 cup fruit—70 calories; with lemonade or rosé—80 calories, or with dry sherry—85 calories.)

SPARKLING FRUIT IN WINE

The mandarin-orange version is pictured on page 54.

For each serving, place ¼ cup fresh fruit in goblet. Pour ⅓ cup wine over fruit. Serve immediately.

Combinations

Cantaloupe balls or mandarin orange segments and Chianti.
1 serving/75 calories.

Strawberries or peach slices and rosé.
1 serving/75 calories.

Pineapple tidbits or seedless green grapes and Rhine wine.
1 serving/75 calories with pineapple; 85 calories with grapes.

FRESH PINEAPPLE TROPICALE

Pour ¼ cup orange-flavored liqueur on 3 cups cut-up fresh pineapple and toss. Divide among 6 dessert dishes and garnish each with a sprig of mint.

6 servings/75 calories each.

WATERMELON CRYSTALS

2 cups sieved watermelon pulp
  (about 4 cups diced)
1 can (6 ounces) frozen lemonade
  concentrate, partially thawed
1 lemonade can water

2 egg whites
¼ cup sugar
3 or 4 drops red food color
6 watermelon balls
Mint leaves

Pretty as a picture. As a shortcut, liquefy melon in your blender.

Mix watermelon pulp, lemonade concentrate and water; pour into refrigerator tray. Freeze until mushy, 1½ to 2 hours (do not freeze until firm).

Beat egg whites in small mixer bowl until foamy. Beat in sugar, 1 tablespoon at a time; beat until stiff and glossy. Do not underbeat. Place watermelon mixture in chilled bowl; fold in meringue and food color. Turn into 2 refrigerator trays. Freeze, stirring once or twice, until firm. Serve in dessert dishes; garnish each serving with a watermelon ball and mint leaves.

6 servings/110 calories each.

Variations

Cantaloupe Crystals: Substitute 2 cups sieved cantaloupe pulp (about 1 medium) for the watermelon pulp and add 2 drops yellow food color. (6 servings/80 calories each.)

Honeydew Crystals: Substitute 2 cups sieved honeydew melon pulp for the watermelon pulp and green food color for the red food color. (6 servings/80 calories each.)

HOMEMADE LIME SHERBET

¾ cup boiling water
1 envelope low-calorie lime-flavored
  gelatin
½ cup sugar

1½ cups buttermilk
1½ teaspoons grated lemon peel
3 tablespoons lemon juice

Pictured on page 38.

Pour boiling water on gelatin and sugar in small mixer bowl; stir until gelatin and sugar are dissolved. Stir in remaining ingredients. Place in freezer until thickened but not set.

Beat until fluffy; pour into refrigerator tray and freeze until firm.

8 servings/70 calories each. (Each serving: ½ cup.)

LAST-MINUTE ANGEL FOOD CAKE TOPPINGS

Evaporated Milk Topping

⅔ cup evaporated skim milk   2 teaspoons lemon juice
¼ cup sugar

Pour skim milk into small mixer bowl; place in freezer until ice crystals form around edge, about 30 minutes. Add sugar and lemon juice; beat until very thick and fluffy. Serve immediately. (Topping can also be refrigerated up to 1 hour or frozen for future use.)

2 cups/10 calories per tablespoon.

Egg White-Dry Milk Topping

½ cup nonfat dry milk   1 tablespoon lemon juice
½ cup iced water   ¼ cup sugar
1 egg white   ½ teaspoon vanilla

In small mixer bowl, beat dry milk, iced water and egg white on high speed 3 minutes. Add lemon juice; beat on high speed 1 minute. Beat in sugar, 1 tablespoon at a time; beat until very thick and fluffy. Blend in vanilla on low speed. Serve immediately. (Topping can also be refrigerated up to 1 hour or frozen for future use.)

4 cups/5 calories per tablespoon.

ORANGE-COCONUT ANGEL

Prepare 1 package (15 or 16 ounces) angel food cake mix as directed except—fold in 2 tablespoons grated orange peel and 2 tablespoons flaked coconut with the flour-sugar mixture. Invert tube pan on funnel; let hang until cake is completely cool. Cut cake into 12 or 16 slices.

16 servings/115 calories each; 12 servings/155 calories each.

Get a new generation off on the right foot in eating. Reward with love, console with understanding, use food only to allay hunger.

ORANGE FLUFF ANGEL

2 eggs, beaten
¼ cup sugar
⅓ cup orange juice
1 tablespoon grated orange peel

1 envelope (about 2 ounces)
  dessert topping mix
10-inch angel food cake

Pictured on page 53.

Cook eggs, sugar and orange juice over low heat, stirring constantly, until mixture thickens, about 10 minutes. Remove from heat; stir in orange peel and cool.

Prepare topping mix as directed on package except—substitute skim milk for the milk. Fold orange mixture into topping. Refrigerate at least 1 hour.

Cut cake into 16 slices; top each slice with 2 tablespoons orange topping.

16 servings/145 calories each.

DANISH STRAWBERRY PIE WITH RICE CRUST

1 teaspoon butter or margarine
1 cup cooked regular rice
½ teaspoon vanilla
1 egg white
1 package (4¾ ounces) strawberry-
  flavored pudding and pie filling

1½ teaspoons grated lemon peel
1 quart strawberries
½ cup frozen whipped topping
  (thawed)

Pictured on page 55. Prepare early in the day so the glaze will have time to set.

Bargain bonus. A tablespoon of commercial whipped topping costs a mere 10-15 calories or even less. Check labels for accurate counts.

Heat oven to 350°. Grease 9-inch pie pan with butter. Beat rice, vanilla and egg white with fork. Turn mixture into pie pan; spread evenly with rubber scraper on bottom and halfway up side of pie pan. (Do not leave any holes.) Bake 5 minutes. Cool.

Prepare pudding and pie filling as directed on package for pie filling. Stir in lemon peel; cool.

If strawberries are large, cut into halves. Arrange in pie shell. Carefully pour strawberry filling over strawberries. Refrigerate at least 6 hours. Run knife around edge to loosen crust. Cut into wedges and top each wedge with 1 tablespoon whipped topping.

8 servings/130 calories each.

CUSTARD PIE WITH RICE CRUST

Skim milk in the custard, rice as a crust and you've trimmed 100 calories or more a serving from the traditional custard pie.

1 teaspoon butter or margarine	½ cup sugar
1 cup cooked regular rice	¼ teaspoon salt
¼ teaspoon cinnamon	2 cups skim milk, scalded
1 egg white	½ teaspoon vanilla
2 eggs plus 1 egg yolk	Nutmeg

Heat oven to 350°. Grease 9-inch pie pan with butter. Beat rice, cinnamon and egg white with fork. Turn mixture into pie pan; spread evenly with rubber scraper on bottom and halfway up side of pie pan. (Do not leave any holes.) Bake 5 minutes.

Beat eggs, egg yolk, sugar, salt, skim milk and vanilla thoroughly. Carefully pour into hot rice crust. Sprinkle with nutmeg. Bake until knife inserted 1 inch from edge comes out clean, about 25 minutes. Immediately run knife around edge to loosen crust. Cool.

8 servings/135 calories each.

Substitutions

For the cinnamon: ¼ teaspoon nutmeg, mace, almond extract or vanilla.

FROZEN LEMON GINGER PIE

1 teaspoon butter or margarine	1 cup frozen whipped topping (thawed)
⅓ cup fine gingersnap or vanilla wafer crumbs (about 6 cookies)	1 tablespoon grated lemon peel
3 eggs, separated	¼ cup lemon juice
½ cup sugar	

Pictured on page 53:
Fruit-Cheese Buffet (110),
Frozen Lemon Ginger Pie (130),
Tinted Angel Macaroons (75),
Orange Fluff Angel (145),
Danish Strawberry Pie with Rice Crust (130),
Cocoa Mini-meringues (60).

Grease 9-inch pie pan with butter; sprinkle ¼ cup of the crumbs on bottom and side of pie pan. Beat egg whites until foamy. Beat in sugar, 1 tablespoon at a time; beat until stiff and glossy. Do not underbeat. Beat egg yolks until thick and lemon colored. Fold into meringue. Mix whipped topping, lemon peel and lemon juice; fold into egg mixture. Pour into pie pan; sprinkle remaining crumbs on top. Freeze until firm, 3 to 4 hours. Remove from freezer 10 minutes before serving.

8 servings/130 calories each.

MAPLE FRANGO

½ cup evaporated skim milk
4 egg yolks
½ cup maple-flavored syrup

½ teaspoon vanilla
Chocolate Curls (below) or
    dash instant coffee

A frozen delight that tastes like pure cream but (of course) isn't. Use leftover egg whites for Frozen Almond Meringue (page 58).

Pour skim milk into bowl; place in freezer until ice crystals form around edge, about 30 minutes.

While milk chills, beat egg yolks in small mixer bowl until thick and lemon colored. Heat syrup just to boiling. Pour about half the hot syrup very slowly in a thin stream into egg yolks, beating constantly on medium speed. Stir egg yolk mixture into syrup in pan. Cook over low heat, stirring constantly, until slightly thickened. Cool.

Beat milk and vanilla until very thick and fluffy. Fold in egg yolk mixture. Pour into refrigerator tray. Freeze until firm, at least 4 hours. Cut into 6 servings and garnish each with a Chocolate Curl.

6 servings / 125 calories each.

Chocolate Curls

With vegetable parer or sharp thin knife, cut across block of semisweet or unsweetened chocolate with long thin strokes.

CHOCOLATE MINT SNOWCAPS

1 envelope (about 2 ounces) dessert
    topping mix
¼ teaspoon peppermint extract

1 drop green or red food color
1 can (18 ounces) chocolate fudge
    pudding

Prepare topping mix as directed on package except—substitute skim milk for the milk and peppermint extract for the vanilla. Remove ½ cup of the topping to small bowl; fold in food color. Fold pudding into remaining topping.

Divide pudding mixture among 8 dessert dishes; top each with 1 tablespoon colored topping. Freeze no longer than 2 hours. Remove from freezer 15 minutes before serving.

8 servings / 120 calories each. (Each serving: ½ cup.)

Pictured on page 54:
Fast Frozen Fruit (125),
Chocolate Mint Snowcaps (120),
Raspberry De-luscious (105),
Frozen Almond Meringue (90),
Sparkling Fruit in Wine (75).

POTS DE CREME

Chocolate-flecked puddings —each is minus nearly 100 calories from its traditional counterpart. Pictured on the cover.

¾ cup evaporated skim milk
⅓ cup sugar
¼ cup cocoa
1 teaspoon unflavored gelatin

⅛ teaspoon salt
1 egg, beaten
⅓ cup evaporated skim milk
1 teaspoon vanilla
Frozen whipped topping (thawed)

Pour ¾ cup skim milk into small mixer bowl; place in freezer until ice crystals form around edge, about 30 minutes.

Mix sugar, cocoa, gelatin, salt, egg and ⅓ cup skim milk in small saucepan until smooth. Cook over low heat, stirring constantly, until slightly thickened, about 5 minutes. Remove from heat; stir in vanilla and set aside.

Beat chilled milk on high speed until very thick and fluffy. Carefully fold in cocoa mixture, 1 tablespoon at a time. Divide among 8 demitasse cups or small dessert dishes. Refrigerate no longer than 1 hour. Top each with 1 teaspoon whipped topping.

8 servings/85 calories each.

COCOA MALLOW

Mix iced tea and low-calorie ginger ale for a sparkly summer cooler.

8 large marshmallows
¾ cup skim milk
2 tablespoons cocoa
½ teaspoon vanilla

Dash salt
1 envelope (about 2 ounces) dessert
  topping mix

Heat marshmallows, skim milk and cocoa in small saucepan over medium heat, stirring constantly, until marshmallows are melted. Stir in vanilla and salt. Let stand at room temperature about 30 minutes.

Prepare topping mix as directed on package except—substitute skim milk for the milk. Reserve 2 tablespoons of the topping; fold cocoa mixture into remaining topping just until mixture is marbled. Divide among 6 dessert dishes. Top each with 1 teaspoon reserved topping. Refrigerate about 1 hour.

6 servings/125 calories each.

FROSTY EGGNOGS

2 **eggs, separated**
Dash salt
¼ **cup light rum or 1**
  tablespoon rum flavoring

1 **carton (4½ ounces) frozen**
  whipped topping (thawed)
Nutmeg

Spoon-up eggnog, Southern style. Pictured on page 39.

Beat egg whites until stiff. Beat egg yolks and salt in small mixer bowl until thick and lemon colored, about 5 minutes. Stir in rum. Fold whipped topping into egg yolks, then fold in whites. Divide among 6 cups; sprinkle with nutmeg and freeze. Remove from freezer 10 minutes before serving.

6 servings/75 calories each with rum flavoring; 95 calories each with rum. (Each serving: ½ cup.)

INDIVIDUAL APRICOT CHEESECAKES

2 **eggs, separated**
½ **cup sugar**
1½ **packages (8-ounce size)**
  Neufchâtel cheese, softened

1 **teaspoon vanilla**
8 **dried apricots, finely chopped**
2 **tablespoons apricot preserves**

Lower-calorie Neufchâtel cheese and an absence of crust put these rich treats within the calorie-counter's reach.

Heat oven to 350°. Line 12 medium muffin cups with paper baking cups. Beat egg whites in small mixer bowl until foamy. Beat in sugar, 1 tablespoon at a time; beat until stiff and glossy. Do not underbeat.

In large mixer bowl, blend cheese, egg yolks and vanilla on low speed, scraping bowl constantly, 1 minute. Beat on high speed, scraping bowl occasionally, until mixture is smooth and fluffy, about 2 minutes. Stir in apricots. Fold meringue into cheese mixture. Divide among muffin cups. Bake until knife inserted in center of one comes out clean, about 20 minutes. Refrigerate until serving time.

Remove paper cups and top each serving with ½ teaspoon apricot preserves.

12 servings/145 calories each.

NOTE: Cheesecakes can be frozen up to 2 weeks. Remove to refrigerator about 20 minutes before serving.

FROZEN ALMOND MERINGUE

Snowy base for your favorite fruit. Pictured on page 54. For greater volume, bring egg whites to room temperature before you beat them; refrigerate leftover yolks (no longer than a few days) to make Maple Frango (page 55).

4 **egg whites**
¼ **cup sugar**
1 **envelope (about 2 ounces) dessert topping mix**

1 **teaspoon almond extract**
4½ **cups fresh fruit (strawberries, peaches, blueberries and/or raspberries)**

Beat egg whites in large mixer bowl until foamy. Beat in sugar, 1 tablespoon at a time; beat until stiff but not dry. Prepare topping mix as directed on package except—substitute skim milk for the milk. Fold topping and almond extract into egg whites. Turn into ungreased baking pan, 8 × 8 × 2 inches. Freeze until firm, at least 4 hours. Cut into 9 squares; top each square with ½ cup fruit.

9 servings/90 calories each.

FAST FROZEN FRUIT

Pictured on page 54.

1 **envelope unflavored gelatin**
3 **tablespoons water**
1 **can (6 ounces) frozen orange juice concentrate, partially thawed**
1 **cup nonfat dry milk**
1 **tablespoon sugar**
1 **banana, sliced**

1 **can (8 ounces) crushed pineapple in unsweetened pineapple juice, drained**
1 **can (16 ounces) fruit cocktail in water pack, drained**
Mint leaves

Sprinkle gelatin on water to soften. Heat over medium heat, stirring constantly, until gelatin is dissolved, about 3 minutes.

In small mixer bowl, beat orange juice concentrate and dry milk on low speed 1 minute, scraping bowl occasionally. Beat on high speed until smooth and fluffy. Gradually beat in gelatin and sugar; beat until very thick.

Fold in banana, pineapple and fruit cocktail. Pour into baking pan, 8 × 8 × 2 inches. Freeze until firm, about 2 hours. Remove to refrigerator ½ hour before serving. Cut into 9 servings. Garnish with mint leaves.

9 servings/125 calories each.

ROCKY ROAD CHEESE FRUIT WHIP

1 envelope low-calorie lime-
flavored gelatin
¾ cup 2% cottage cheese
1 carton (4½ ounces) frozen
whipped topping (thawed)
1 drop green food color (optional)

1 cup honeydew melon balls
1 can (8 ounces) crushed pineapple
in unsweetened pineapple juice,
drained
2 tablespoons snipped mint leaves

To vary the color and flavor
use cherry-, strawberry- or
orange-flavored gelatin.
Pictured on page 23.

Sprinkle gelatin on cottage cheese to soften. Stir in and let stand
a few minutes. Stir again until gelatin is dissolved. Fold in whipped
topping, food color and fruits. Cover and refrigerate until serving
time. Divide among 6 dessert dishes and garnish with mint leaves.

6 servings/125 calories each.

RASPBERRY DE-LUSCIOUS

1 package (10 ounces) frozen
raspberries, thawed and drained
(reserve syrup)
1 tablespoon lemon juice

½ cup sugar
1 egg white
1 carton (4½ ounces) frozen
whipped topping (thawed)

Pictured on page 54.

Place raspberries in small mixer bowl. Measure reserved raspberry
syrup; set aside ½ cup and pour remaining syrup into bowl. Add
remaining ingredients except whipped topping; beat on low speed
1 minute. Beat on high speed, scraping bowl occasionally, until
mixture is thick and fluffy, about 3 minutes. Fold in 1 cup of the
whipped topping. Spread in ungreased baking pan, 8 × 8 × 2 inches.
Freeze until firm, about 2 hours.

Just before serving, fold reserved ½ cup raspberry syrup into the
remaining whipped topping. Cut dessert into squares and top each
with about 2 tablespoons topping.

9 servings/105 calories each.

Variation

Peach De-luscious: Substitute 1 package (10 ounces) frozen peach
slices for the frozen raspberries; sprinkle nutmeg over each serving.
(9 servings/105 calories each.)

COCOA MINI-MERINGUES

Three of these little confections, filling and all, have only 60 calories. Pictured on page 53.

3 egg whites
¼ teaspoon cream of tartar
¾ cup sugar
2 tablespoons cocoa

Frozen whipped topping (thawed)
Fresh fruit, semisweet chocolate
pieces or maraschino cherries

Heat oven to 275°. Cover 2 baking sheets with aluminum foil. Beat egg whites and cream of tartar in small mixer bowl until foamy. Beat in sugar, 1 tablespoon at a time; beat until stiff and glossy. Do not underbeat. Sprinkle cocoa on meringue and gently fold in.

Drop meringue by level measuring-tablespoonfuls about 1½ inches apart onto baking sheets. Make small indentation in center of each with tip of teaspoon. Bake 10 minutes. Turn off oven; leave meringues in oven with door closed 1 hour. Remove from oven; finish cooling meringues away from draft.

Top each meringue with 1 teaspoon whipped topping and 1 piece fresh fruit. Wrap leftover plain or topped meringues in aluminum foil and freeze up to 2 weeks.

48 meringues/20 calories each.

Variation

Three-in-One Meringues: Omit cocoa; divide meringue into 3 parts (about 1 cup each). Fold into each part one of the following:
   ¼ teaspoon powdered instant coffee
   2 teaspoons cocoa
   ½ teaspoon grated orange or lemon peel
   4 drops food color
   ¼ teaspoon almond or peppermint extract

TINTED ANGEL MACAROONS

1 package (16 ounces) one-step
  angel food cake mix
½ cup low-calorie strawberry- or
  orange-flavored soda pop
  (no sugar)

1½ teaspoons almond extract
1 package (7 ounces) cookie
  coconut (about 2 cups)

Heat oven to 350°. Cover baking sheet with aluminum foil or heavy brown paper. In large mixer bowl, blend cake mix, soda pop and almond extract on low speed, scraping bowl constantly, ½ minute. Beat on medium speed, scraping bowl occasionally, 1 minute. Fold in coconut. Drop batter by measuring-teaspoonfuls about 2 inches apart onto baking sheet. Bake until set, 10 to 12 minutes. Slide foil, with cookies, onto wire rack; cool cookies completely before removing from foil. Store cookies in freezer or between layers of waxed paper in a box.

About 8 dozen cookies/25 calories each.

Variation

Fruit Macaroons: Substitute water for the soda pop, vanilla for the almond extract and 1 cup chopped dried apricots, figs or prunes for the coconut. (About 8 dozen cookies/25 calories each.)

If you want to save time by making these larger, drop them by ordinary teaspoonfuls; you'll get 6 dozen, at 35 calories each. Pictured on page 53.

SOUR LEMON COOKIES

Heat oven to 375°. Prepare 1 package (18.5 ounces) yellow cake mix as directed except—decrease water to ½ cup and beat just until ingredients are mixed. Drop batter by measuring-teaspoonfuls 2 inches apart onto greased baking sheet. Bake until light brown on edges, 6 to 8 minutes. Immediately remove from baking sheet and cool on wire rack. Spread ½ teaspoon Lemon Glaze (below) on each cookie.

About 8 dozen cookies/40 calories each.

Lemon Glaze

Mix 2 cups confectioners' sugar, 2 tablespoons grated lemon peel and ¼ cup lemon juice until smooth.

Variation: For chocolate cookies (only 30 calories each), use the same size package of devils food cake mix, omit glaze and drop a dab (¼ teaspoon) of canned dark Dutch fudge frosting on top of each cookie.

ROOT BEER IN THE CLOUDS

For each serving, place ⅓ cup Dry Milk Whip (below) or Evaporated Milk Whip (page 45) in tall glass. Pour ½ can (12-ounce size) chilled low-calorie root beer (no sugar) into glass. Serve immediately.

1 serving/30 calories.

Dry Milk Whip

½ teaspoon unflavored gelatin
2 tablespoons sugar
3 tablespoons nonfat dry milk
½ cup water
½ teaspoon vanilla

Mix gelatin, sugar and dry milk in small saucepan. Stir in water. Heat over medium heat, stirring until gelatin is dissolved, about 3 minutes. Stir in vanilla. Pour into small mixer bowl. Refrigerate until slightly thickened.

Beat on high speed until stiff peaks form. Serve immediately. (Or topping can be refrigerated up to 1 hour or frozen for making Root Beer in the Clouds [above] or Rosy Peaches Flambé [page 45].) (2 cups/5 calories per tablespoon.)

FOAMING SODA POP

For each serving, fill tall glass ⅓ full with chilled low-calorie favorite-flavored soda pop (no sugar). Stir in 2 tablespoons nonfat dry milk (it will foam up and fill the glass). Serve immediately. Pour in additional soda pop as needed.

1 serving/30 calories.

Just be sure the low-calorie soda pop you use for these recipes is carbonated!

BREAKFAST IS A CALORIE-COUNTER'S MOST IMPORTANT MEAL

Never skip breakfast! You need it to keep you going during the day; you'll have the rest of the day to "work it off." It should provide at least one-fourth of your day's nutritional needs (see page 6).

Fruits, Beverages	Calories	Fruits, Beverages	Calories
1 medium grapefruit half	50	4 ounces unsweetened pineapple juice	70
1 medium orange	75	4 ounces tomato juice	25
1 cantaloupe half (5-inch diameter)	60		
4 ounces orange juice	55	8 ounces skim milk	90
4 ounces apricot nectar	70	Coffee or tea	0

Meats, Cereals, Breads	Calories	Meats, Cereals, Breads	Calories
1 cup corn flake cereal	100	1 slice Canadian-style bacon	65
1 cup presweetened corn flake cereal	155	1 egg, boiled or poached	80
		1 slice toast	65
1 cup whole wheat flake cereal	105	1 slice French toast	185
½ cup oatmeal	65	1 four-inch pancake	60

Extras	Calories	Extras	Calories
1 teaspoon sugar	15	1 tablespoon low-calorie syrup	2
1 teaspoon butter or margarine	35	1 tablespoon Calorie-saving Grape Jelly (page 64)	5

NOTE: Avoid bacon, fried eggs (except those fried in skillet coated with vegetable spray-on for cookware), coffee cakes, doughnuts and jelly or jam—they're all high in calories! Reduce calories in French toast and pancakes (see chart) by using skim milk and coating the griddle with vegetable spray-on for cookware.

A Cram Course in Calorie-Cutting

or

What You Can Eat When

No two ways about it, cutting calories takes a bit of doing. It's rather like enrolling in a college course. Just signing up isn't enough—you still have to do the homework and show up for classes. In this chapter we give you an outline of the curriculum—guidelines for breakfast (very significant), required reading for lunch at home or on the job, a few formulas for party plans. And for those inevitable moments of yawning emptiness there's a list of sturdy stopgaps with calories counted and a sketch of high-calorie traps—all calculated to earn you an A in your slimming course.

I carry my lunch. How can I save calories?

LOW-CALORIE BROWN BAG LUNCH

Add color, sparkle and crunch to your lunch with fresh fruit . . . crisp vegetable snack or pickled vegetables (page 35) . . . cherry tomatoes with shaker of lemon pepper . . . kabob of cooked meat, cheese and fruit or vegetable . . . melba toast open-face sandwich (page 65) . . . hot soup or vegetable in widemouthed vacuum bottle . . . cottage cheese or cold salad makings with low-calorie dressing in leakproof pill bottle . . . low-calorie pudding . . . cookie (page 61) . . . fortified skim milk.

LACY MELBA TOAST

Place unsliced 1-pound loaf Vienna white bread or rye bread in freezer 1 hour. Cut with electric knife into thin slices (⅛ to ¼ inch). If desired, cut each slice into halves or thirds.

Heat oven to 325°. Arrange slices in single layer on ungreased baking sheet. If desired, sprinkle some slices with garlic salt, onion salt or ¼ teaspoon cinnamon-sugar (mixture of 1 tablespoon sugar and ½ teaspoon cinnamon). Bake until crisp and golden brown around edges, 12 to 15 minutes. Toast can be packed in box and used as needed.

60 slices/20 calories each; 25 calories each with cinnamon-sugar.

CRUNCHY COTTAGE CHEESE

1 carton (12 ounces)
    2% cottage cheese (1½ cups)
½ green pepper, finely chopped, or
    ½ cup chopped celery
	1 dill pickle, finely chopped
	1 tablespoon freeze-dried
	    chives
	Salt

Mix cottage cheese, green pepper, dill pickle and chives; season with salt. Nice to spread on slices of unbuttered dark bread (60 calories each) or on small melba toast rounds (8 calories each).

1¾ cups/15 calories per tablespoon. (Makes enough for 6 to 8 slices bread.)

OPEN-FACE CHICKEN SANDWICH

Spread 1½ teaspoons low-calorie Thousand Island dressing on thin slice French or Vienna bread. Top with slices of smoked chicken (1 ounce). Garnish with 1 teaspoon currant jelly and several Pickled Cucumber slices (page 35).

1 sandwich/110 calories.

OPEN-FACE PORK SANDWICH

Mix 1 tablespoon applesauce and ⅛ teaspoon horseradish; spread on thin slice rye bread. Top with thin slice cooked pork roast (1 ounce) and sprinkle with salt. Garnish with 3 pimiento-stuffed olive slices.

1 sandwich/135 calories.

CALORIE-SAVING GRAPE JELLY

1 cup unsweetened grape juice
1 cup low-calorie grape-flavored
   soda pop (no sugar)

1 envelope unflavored gelatin
1 or 2 drops red food color
   (optional)

Measure grape juice and soda pop into small saucepan. Sprinkle gelatin on liquid to soften. Stir over medium heat until gelatin is dissolved, about 3 minutes. Heat to boiling. Stir in food color. Immediately pour into two 1-cup jelly glasses. Cool. Cover and refrigerate until thickened. Store in refrigerator; keep no longer than 3 weeks.

2 glasses/5 calories per tablespoon.

MOCK MAYONNAISE

1 carton (8 ounces) unflavored
   yogurt (1 cup)
2 tablespoons mayonnaise

¼ teaspoon salt
Dash paprika
1 drop yellow food color

Mix all ingredients with rotary beater until smooth. Cover and refrigerate 2 hours before serving.

About 1 cup/20 calories per tablespoon.

Brown-bag the foods you're allowed for lunch (page 6). Count calories before they go into the bag.

HEARTY VEGETABLE SOUP

I'm at home for lunch—everything tempts me. What's a good way to hold calories down?

2 cans (12 ounces each) vegetable juice cocktail
2 cups water
1 small cabbage (about 1 pound), finely chopped
1 medium onion, sliced

3 small or 2 medium carrots, sliced
½ cup chopped celery
2 tablespoons instant beef or chicken bouillon

Heat all ingredients to boiling. Reduce heat; cover and simmer 1 hour.

8 servings/45 calories each. (Each serving: 1 cup.)

NOTE: Cabbage can be chopped in blender. Cut cabbage into 2-inch pieces. Place half the pieces in blender; cover with water and chop, watching carefully. Drain thoroughly. Repeat with remaining cabbage.

GERMAN-STYLE VEGETABLE SOUP

3 cups reserved pork broth*
1 can (8 ounces) sauerkraut
1 bay leaf
½ to 1 teaspoon salt
1 cup thinly sliced carrot

1 cup diagonal slices celery
2 medium tomatoes, peeled and cut into wedges
¼ cup barley
2 tablespoons snipped parsley

Skim fat from broth. Cut through sauerkraut (while it's still in the can) with kitchen scissors. Heat broth, sauerkraut (with liquid) and remaining ingredients except parsley to boiling. Reduce heat; cover and cook until carrot is tender, 25 to 30 minutes. Remove bay leaf. Serve in soup bowls and sprinkle with parsley.

6 servings/70 calories each. (Each serving: 1 cup.)

* Reserved broth from Pork Roll (page 15); if necessary, add water to measure 3 cups. Canned chicken broth or beef broth (bouillon) can be substituted for the pork broth.

QUICK SPINACH SOUP

2½ cups water
1 tablespoon instant beef or
  chicken bouillon
1 package (10 ounces) frozen
  chopped spinach
1 can (4 ounces) mushroom stems
  and pieces

1 jar (2 ounces) sliced pimiento,
  drained
½ teaspoon garlic salt
Dash rosemary leaves
Thin unpared cucumber slices or
  5 tablespoons unflavored yogurt

Heat water, bouillon and spinach to boiling; break spinach apart with fork. Cover and cook until tender, about 3 minutes. Stir in mushrooms (with liquid), pimiento, garlic salt and rosemary leaves; heat. Divide among 5 soup bowls and garnish each with cucumber slices or yogurt.

5 servings/30 calories each. (Each serving: 1 cup.)

ROSY CONSOMME

3½ cups water
1 tablespoon plus 1 teaspoon
  instant beef bouillon or 4 cubes
  beef bouillon

1 cup tomato juice
6 unpared cucumber slices

Heat all ingredients except cucumber slices to boiling, stirring occasionally. Serve hot in cups—or let consommé cool; serve in cups over ice. Garnish each with a cucumber slice.

6 servings/10 calories each. (Each serving: ¾ cup.)

NIPPY APPETIZER SOUP

1¼ cups water
2 teaspoons instant beef bouillon
  or 2 cubes beef bouillon
1½ teaspoons horseradish

1 teaspoon lemon juice
¼ teaspoon dill weed
5 thin lemon slices

Heat all ingredients except lemon slices to boiling, stirring occasionally. Serve hot in cups and garnish each with a thin lemon slice.

5 servings/5 calories each. (Each serving: ½ cup.)

Fill up on a 5-minute soup or an open-face sandwich (page 65). Or treat yourself to a lunch under 300 calories (page 41).

How can I count calories when I buy my lunch?

Go to a cafeteria when possible—eyes forward past the desserts. Choose meats without gravy . . . salads with lemon juice instead of dressing . . . clear or vegetable soups. If hamburger is your choice, ask for it on unbuttered toast (65 calories versus 120 for a bun). Avoid lunch counter desserts; bring an orange or apple to eat at coffee time instead. Carry vegetable snacks to fill up on before or after lunch.

How can I count calories at a friend's dinner party without losing the friend?

Save your calories before the big dinner. Offer to bring some food for the dinner, then furnish a low-calorie addition to the menu (maybe a low-calorie fruit and melon boat). Serve yourself smaller portions of rich foods, giant helpings of salads and vegetables. Ask for a smaller dessert, then leave some on your plate. Suggest an after-dinner walk or game of table tennis. Get out the jump rope after you get home. Cut down on calories the next day.

FRUIT KABOBS IN WATERMELON BOAT

1 round watermelon	¾ pound dark sweet cherries
1 medium cantaloupe	1 pint strawberries
1 can (15¼ ounces) pineapple chunks in unsweetened pineapple juice, drained	

Cut watermelon horizontally in half, making saw-toothed edge with sharp thin knife; cut melon balls from top half. Cut thin slice from bottom half so watermelon will stand upright. Remove fruit from bottom half to just below saw-toothed edge.

Cut balls from cantaloupe. On each of about 40 bamboo skewers, place watermelon ball, cantaloupe ball, pineapple chunk, cherry and strawberry. Insert kabobs upright in watermelon boat.

About 20 servings/100 calories each. (Each serving: 2 kabobs.)

Try some fake-out drinks. Drink iced coffee, tea or water in a fancy glass with an orange slice or bruised mint. Away from home, ask for club soda (no calories) with a twist of lime, a bloody Mary without the vodka (cutting calories to 60 for 6 ounces) or a screwdriver without vodka (about 90 calories for the orange juice alone).

How can I avoid alcoholic drinks without calling attention to my weight problem?

Strictly as an extra! Two 3½-ounce Manhattans cost 230 calories; two martinis, 280; two beers, 230. A 1½-ounce jigger of liquor adds about 100 calories to any mixed drink, to say nothing of salted peanuts (460 calories for ½ cup) and other high-calorie snacks that accompany a drink.

How does a drink fit into my eating plan?

Try your favorite drink stretched with low-calorie soda. Or drink whisky with water or soda with lots of ice for a long drink.

But sometimes I really feel like a drink!

WINE SNOWBALL

Freeze ⅔ cup dry red wine and 1⅓ cups low-calorie ginger ale (no sugar) or club soda in refrigerator tray until mushy, about 2 hours. Spoon into 2 sherbet dishes; garnish each with a strawberry.

2 servings/65 calories each. (Each serving: 1 cup.)

WINE WITH FRUIT KABOB

For each serving, pour ⅓ cup dry red wine and ⅔ cup low-calorie ginger ale (no sugar) into tall glass. Add ice cubes or crushed ice to fill glass. Place 2 seedless green grapes, 1 pineapple chunk and 1 strawberry on bamboo skewer; place in glass.

1 serving/70 calories.

WINE COOLER WITH CHEESE AND CRACKERS

For each serving, pour ¼ cup chilled dry red wine and ½ cup chilled club soda into goblet. Serve with 1 soda cracker, 2 melba toast rounds, ⅓ ounce Camembert cheese and ⅓ ounce pasteurized Neufchâtel cheese spread.

1 serving/125 calories.

I'm having guests for dinner. *They* aren't counting calories! What shall I do?

Ah—now's your challenge and your opportunity! Plan a low-calorie dinner so colorful and good tasting no one will think about calories. Then figure out your allowed calories, watch your own portions, and enjoy!

SAMPLE MENUS

TEENAGE KITCHEN PARTY
8 servings/375 calories each

Cantaloupe Wedges (¼ melon each serving, 5 inches in diameter)
Chili with Yellow Beans (double recipe, page 12)
Mexican Salad (page 34)
Cloverleaf Rolls (1 roll, 1 teaspoon butter each serving)
Root Beer in the Clouds (page 62)

COZY FIRESIDE DINNER
6 servings/420 calories each

Antipasto Tray: Garlic Pickles, Vegetable Snacks (page 37), Pickled Artichokes (page 35)
Chicken with Mushroom Gravy (page 21)
Spinach Salad (1 cup each serving) with Lemon Wedges
Baked Potatoes (1 small, 1 tablespoon Convertible Potato Topper each serving, page 44)
Rosy Peaches Flambé (page 45)

CALORIE-COUNTER'S LUNCHEON
8 servings/400 calories each

Dilled Fish Sticks (triple recipe, page 26)
Gazpacho Mold (page 33)
Spinach Continental (double recipe, page 43)
Rye Wafers (3 wafers each serving)
Fruit-Cheese Buffet (page 47)

CELEBRATION SUPPER
8 servings/380 calories each

Party Round Steak (page 9)
Crisp Vegetable Snacks (page 37)
Poppy Seed Noodles (½ cup each serving, page 18)
Asparagus Cuts (½ cup each serving)
Melba Toast Rounds (2 rounds each serving)
Pots de Crème (page 56)

COUNT THE CALORIES AHEAD OF TIME

Before you take your first bite, remember . . .

Calories in:	Equal Calories in:
1 chocolate éclair (315)	■ 5 cantaloupe halves
1 chocolate malt (500)	■ 14 fresh peaches
1 slice (1/16) 2-layer, 9-inch chocolate cake, frosted (235)	■ 4 cups fresh strawberries
½ cup salted peanuts (460)	■ 18 cups salted popcorn
1 tablespoon peanut butter (95)	■ 1 cup unsweetened applesauce (try as a spread)
1 cup cream of potato soup (185)	■ 37 cups beef bouillon (made from bouillon cubes)
1 glass whole milk (160)	■ 1¾ glasses fortified skim milk

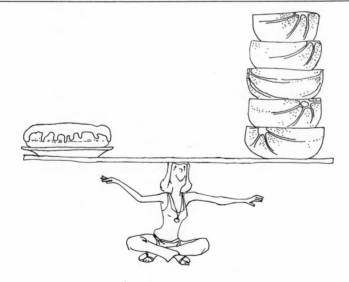

Calorie Chart

Apple (1 med.)	90
Apple juice (½ cup)	60
Applesauce, canned (½ cup)	
sweetened	115
unsweetened	50
Apricots, canned (½ cup)	
sweetened	110
unsweetened	40
Apricots, fresh (3 med.)	55
Asparagus (½ cup)	20
Bacon (2 med. slices)	90
Bacon-flavored vegetable	
protein chips (4 tbsp.)	115
Banana (6″)	80
Beans (½ cup)	
green	15
navy	110
Beef, lean, trimmed (3 oz.)	
chuck	180
corned	185
dried or chipped	175
ground, lean (11% fat)	185
ground, regular	
(20% fat)	245
liver, fried	195
roast, rump	180
steak, flank	170
steak, Porterhouse,	
T-bone	190
steak, round	165
steak, sirloin	175
Beef pot pie (4¼″ diam.)	560
Beer (8 oz.)	115
Beets (½ cup)	25
Biscuit (2″ diam.)	100
Blueberries, fresh (⅓ cup)	30
Bologna (3 x ⅛″ slice)	80
Bread (1 slice)	
French, raisin or rye	60
white or whole wheat	65
Broccoli (½ cup)	20
Brussels sprouts (½ cup)	30
Butter, regular (1 tbsp.)	100
Butter, whipped (1 tbsp.)	65
Buttermilk, skim (8 oz.)	90

Cabbage, raw (½ cup)	10
Cake	
angel (1/12 of	
10″ diam.)	135
chocolate (2-layer,	
chocolate icing,	
1/16 of 9″ diam.)	235
fruit (1/30 of 8″ loaf)	55
pound (½″ slice)	140
sponge (1/12 of	
10″ diam.)	195
yellow (2-layer, chocolate	
icing, 1/16 of 9″ diam.)	275
Cantaloupe (½ of 5″ diam.)	60
Caramel (1 med.)	40
Carbonated beverage (8 oz.)	
cola-type, sweetened	95
fruit-flavored	115
ginger ale	75
low-calorie (refer to label)	
root beer	100
tonic water	80
Carrots, raw or cooked	
(½ cup or one 5″ long)	25
Catsup (1 tbsp.)	15
Cauliflower (½ cup)	15
Celery, raw (8″ stalk)	5
Cereal, cooked (½ cup)	
farina	50
oatmeal	65
Cereal, dry (1 cup)	
bran flakes	105
corn, puffed	100
corn, puffed,	
presweetened	115
corn flakes	100
corn flakes, presweetened	155
oats, puffed	100
wheat flakes	105
wheat germ (3 tbsp.)	100
Cheese	
American (1 oz.)	105
blue or Roquefort (1 oz.)	105
Camembert (1 oz.)	85
Cheddar (1 oz.)	115
cottage, dry curd (¼ cup)	45
cottage, creamed, 2%	
(¼ cup)	45

Cheese (cont.)	
cream (1 oz.)	95
Neufchâtel 1 oz.)	70
Parmesan (1 tbsp.)	25
spread (1 oz.)	80
Swiss (1 oz.)	95
Cherries, canned (½ cup)	
sweetened	90
unsweetened	50
Cherries, fresh (½ cup)	70
Cherry, maraschino (1 large)	10
Chicken	
breast, fried (3 oz.)	170
liver, cooked (1 med.)	75
pot pie (4¼″ diam.)	535
roasted, no skin (3 oz.)	
dark meat	150
light meat	140
salad (3 heaping tbsp.)	185
Chili con carne with beans	
(½ cup)	170
Chili sauce (2 tbsp.)	35
Chocolate bar, plain (1 oz.)	150
Chocolate kisses (7)	150
Clams, canned (3 oz.)	85
Cocoa drink (8 oz.)	245
Coconut, shredded,	
firmly packed (½ cup)	225
Cod, broiled (3 oz.)	145
Coleslaw (½ cup)	55
Cookies	
brownie with nuts (2″ sq.)	145
chocolate chip (1 med.)	50
oatmeal with raisins	
(3″ diam.)	65
sandwich-type (1 med.)	50
sugar (3″ diam.)	90
vanilla wafer (1 med.)	15
Cordials (1 cordial glass)	55-70
Corn bread (2″ sq.)	110
Corn on the cob (5″ ear)	70
Corn, whole kernel (½ cup)	85
Crab (3 oz.)	85
Cranberry sauce,	
sweetened (½ cup)	200
Cucumber, raw (12 slices)	10
Cupcake, plain (2½″ diam.)	90
Custard (½ cup)	150

Dates (3 med.)	80
Deviled ham (1 tbsp.)	45
Doughnut (1 av.)	
cake-type or raised	125
cake-type, sugared	150
raised, jelly center	225
Duck, roasted,	
no skin (3 oz.)	265
Eclair, custard filled,	
chocolate icing (1 av.)	315
Eggplant, raw (2 slices)	25
Egg (1)	80
Fig, dried (1 large)	60
Fish sticks (3 oz.)	150
Frankfurter (2 oz.)	170
French toast (1 slice)	185
Fruit cocktail (½ cup)	
sweetened	75
unsweetened	40
Fudge (1″ sq.)	105
Gelatin, fruit flavored	
(½ cup)	70
Gingerbread (2″ sq.)	205
Graham cracker (2½″ sq.)	30
Grapefruit (½ med.)	50
Grapefruit juice,	
unsweetened (½ cup)	50
Grape juice, canned (½ cup)	80
Grapes (½ cup)	35
Gumdrops (1 large or	
8 small)	35
Halibut, broiled (3 oz.)	145
Hash, canned (½ cup)	
corned beef	230
roast beef	145
Honey (1 tbsp.)	65
Honeydew melon	
(¼ of 5″ diam.)	35
Ice cream, about 10%	
fat (½ cup)	130
Ice cream soda (8 oz.)	260
Ice milk, hardened (½ cup)	100
Ice milk, soft-serve (½ cup)	135
Jams and preserves (1 tbsp.)	55
Jelly (1 tbsp.)	50
Jelly beans (10)	65

Lamb, lean, trimmed (3 oz.)	
chop or roast, leg	160
roast, shoulder	175
Lemonade (½ cup)	55
Lettuce (2 large leaves)	10
Lima beans, dry,	
cooked (1 cup)	260
Liquor, 80-90 proof	
(1½ oz.)	100-110
Lobster (3 oz.)	80
Lollipop (2¼″ diam.)	110
Macaroni and cheese	
(1 cup)	430
Macaroni, cooked (½ cup)	95
Malted milk shake,	
chocolate (8 oz.)	500
Manhattan (3½ oz.)	165
Margarine, low calorie	
(refer to label)	
Margarine, regular (1 tbsp.)	100
Marshmallow (1 large)	25
Martini (3½ oz.)	140
Meat loaf, beef and pork	
(4 x ⅜″ slice)	265
Milk (8 oz.)	
evaporated	345
evaporated skim	190
shake, chocolate	420
skim	90
sweetened condensed	980
2%	145
whole	160
Muffin (3″ diam.)	120
Mushrooms, canned (¼ cup)	10
Mustard, prepared (1 tsp.)	5
Noodles, cooked (½ cup)	100
Nuts (¼ cup)	
cashews, roasted	195
peanuts, dry roasted	210
peanuts, oil roasted	230
pecans	185
walnuts	200
Oil, salad or	
cooking (1 tbsp.)	125
Old-fashioned (4 oz.)	180
Olives, green (4 med.)	15

Olives, ripe (3 small)	15
Onions (½ cup)	30
Orange (1 med.)	75
Orange juice,	
unsweetened (½ cup)	60
Pancake (4″ diam.)	60
Peach, fresh (1 med.)	35
Peaches, canned (½ cup)	
sweetened	100
unsweetened	40
Peanut brittle (2½″ sq.)	110
Peanut butter (4 tbsp.)	380
Pear, fresh (1 med.)	100
Pears, canned (½ cup)	
sweetened	100
unsweetened	40
Peas (½ cup)	
cow, blackeye, dry	95
green	60
split, dry	145
Pepper, green, raw (1 med.)	15
Pickle, dill (1 med.)	10
Pickle, sweet (1 small)	20
Pie (1/7 of 9″ diam.)	
apple, cherry, rhubarb	350
blueberry	330
coconut custard	315
custard	285
lemon meringue	305
mince	365
peach	360
pecan	490
pumpkin	275
Pineapple, canned (1 slice)	
sweetened	90
unsweetened	40
Pineapple, fresh (½ cup diced)	40
Pineapple juice,	
unsweetened (½ cup)	70
Pizza, cheese (5 oz.)	370
Pizza, sausage (7 oz.)	470
Plum, fresh (1 med.)	25
Popcorn, popped (1 cup)	
plain	25
sugar-coated	135
with oil and salt	40
Popover (1 av.)	110
Popsicle (3 oz.)	70

Pork, lean, trimmed
chop (3 oz.)	230
ham, cured (3 oz.)	160
roast, loin (3 oz.)	215
sausage link (3 x ½″)	125
spareribs, roasted (about 6 med.)	245
tenderloin (3 oz.)	205

Pork and beans in sweet sauce, canned (1 cup)	385
Pork and beans in tomato sauce, canned (1 cup)	310
Potato chips, 2″ diam. (10)	115

Potatoes
au gratin (½ cup)	145
cooked (2¼″ diam.)	80
frozen and heated (French fried), 2 x ½″ (10)	125
hashed brown (½ cup)	230
mashed, with milk (½ cup)	65
scalloped (½ cup)	105
sweet (½ cup)	120

Pretzels, stick, small (10)	10
Pretzels, thin, twisted (1)	25
Prune juice (½ cup)	100
Prunes (4 med.)	70

Pudding (½ cup)
chocolate	195
tapioca cream	110
vanilla or rice-raisin	140

Radishes (4 small)	5
Raisins, dry (2 tbsp.)	60
Raspberries, fresh (½ cup)	35
Rhubarb, stewed, sweetened (⅓ cup)	190
Rice, cooked (½ cup)	115

Roll (1 av.)
cloverleaf or pan	85
frankfurter or hamburger	120
hard	155
sweet	180

Rye wafers, whole grain (2)	45

Salad dressing (1 tbsp.)
blue cheese or Roquefort	75
French	65

Salad dressing (cont.)
Italian	90
low-calorie (refer to label)	
mayonnaise	100
Thousand Island	80

Salmon, broiled or
baked (3 oz.)	155
Salmon, canned pink (3 oz.)	120
Saltine cracker (2″ sq.)	15

Sandwich (2 slices bread, 1 tsp. butter)
bacon, lettuce, tomato	280
egg or tuna salad	280
ham salad	320

Sauce (2 tbsp.)
butterscotch	205
cheese	65
chocolate	85
gravy	80
tartar	150
tomato	40
white	50

Sauerkraut (½ cup)	20
Scallops, breaded and fried (3 oz.)	165
Sherbet (½ cup)	130

Shrimp (3 oz.)
canned or cooked	100
French fried	190

Soup, made with milk (1 cup)
clam chowder	210
cream of chicken	180
cream of mushroom	215
cream of shrimp	245
oyster stew	200
tomato	175

Soup, made with water (1 cup)
split pea	145
tomato	90
vegetable beef	80

Spaghetti, cooked (½ cup)	80

Spaghetti, with meatballs and tomato sauce
canned (1 cup)	260
home recipe (1 cup)	330
Spinach (½ cup)	20

Spinach, raw (1 oz.)	10

Squash (½ cup)
summer	15
winter	65

Stew, beef and vegetable (1 cup)	210

Strawberries (½ cup)
fresh	30
frozen, sweetened	140

Sugar
brown (½ cup)	410
confectioners' (1 tbsp.)	30
granulated (1 tbsp.)	40

Syrup (1 tbsp.)
corn, light or dark	60
maple	50

Tangerine (1 med.)	40
Tomato, fresh (1 med.)	40
Tomatoes, canned (½ cup)	25
Tomato juice (½ cup)	25

Tuna (3 oz.)
canned in oil, drained	170
canned in water	110

Turkey, roasted, no skin (3 oz.)	165

Veal, lean, trimmed (3 oz.)
chop	175
cutlet	185
roast	145

Waffle (7″ diam.)	210
Watermelon (4 x 8″ wedge)	115

Wine (3 oz.)
champagne (domestic)	65
muscatel, port, sherry	130-140
sauterne	75
vermouth, dry	75-100
vermouth, sweet	120-135

Worcestershire sauce (2 tbsp.)	25

Yogurt, fruit (½ cup)	120
Yogurt, plain (½ cup)	65

Zwieback (1 piece)	30

Index